STRADDLING the Abyss

STRADDLING *the* Abyss

CREATING SUCCESS THROUGH PERSEVERANCE, TIMING, AND A LITTLE LUCK

JOHN W. BADER, JR.

gatekeeper press

Columbus, Ohio

Straddling the Abyss: Creating Success Through Perseverance, Timing, and a Little Luck

Published by Gatekeeper Press
2167 Stringtown Rd, Suite 109
Columbus, OH 43123-2989
www.GatekeeperPress.com

Copyright © 2019 by John W. Bader, Jr.
All rights reserved. Neither this book, nor any parts within it may be sold or reproduced in any form or by any electronic or mechanical means, including information storage and retrieval systems without permission in writing from the author. The only exception is by a reviewer, who may quote short excerpts in a review.

The editorial work for this book is entirely the product of the author. Gatekeeper Press did not participate in and is not responsible for any aspect of this element.

ISBN (paperback): 9781642377927
eISBN: 9781642377934

Table Of Contents

Acknowledgments 9
Foreword 11
Introduction 15

THE EARLY YEARS

Surviving Nature 23
Wrong Side Of The Tracks 33
Slightly Phobic 39

GROWING UP ... SORT OF

Lessons Learned 51
In The Cross-Hairs 58
Auto Immune 65
Jobs From Hell 73

ADULT ADVENTURES

A Wing And A Prayer 91
Home Invasion 97

TROPICAL MISHAPS

Trouble In Paradise 109
South Of The Border 119
The Rain Forest Below 126

MY REAL-LIFE ADVENTURES ARE TAME IN COMPARISON TO THE NEXT STORY

Life In The Balance 137

Epilogue 143
About the Author 145

"Life truly lived is a risky business, and if one puts up too many fences against risk, one ends by shutting out life itself."

—Kenneth S. Davis

Acknowledgments

One of the pieces of the puzzle in the quest for a full life is to write a memoir and pass it along to your children. While working on this project, I discovered growing up and well into adulthood, my energies were channeled toward an unusually high number of risk-related adventures, sometimes planned and in some cases just plain foolhardy. Equally intriguing was that my attraction to risk carried over to my business career. The measured risks I took helped me to launch a successful business platform.

I acknowledge my parents, who gave my brother and me a long leash to be independent, seize opportunities, and stand up to life's challenges. In returning the favor, I gave my parents stressful days, sleepless nights, and a reason to administer corporal punishment, which they seldom shied away from.

I would also like to acknowledge the countless teachers, coaches, employers, friends, and family members whose wisdom and influence helped keep me somewhat grounded and staying the course. Also the college administrators who predicted a dire future for my business endeavors and are now asking me for donations.

My children, Diana and Johnny, who embraced some of my misadventures and were always ready for the next shoe to drop. And Amy, who handled the most challenging conditions thrust upon her with grace and dignity and who taught us all about determination that we should never to give up.

Finally, I would like to recognize my friend, Eric, who introduced me to his colleague in teaching, Gretchen. Burdened with a serious accident and a great personal loss, she nevertheless pressed on and helped me with the editing and rewrites as we prepared this book for publication.

Foreword

A recent article discussed a declining trend facing young adults when they try to match or exceed the income of their parents. Studies show that children born in the late 1940s and 1950s (Baby Boomers) were nearly 90 percent more likely to ultimately exceed their parents' income than those born in the 1980s, millennials. In that group, fewer than 50 percent would achieve the same goal.

Part of this disparity can be traced to the Great Depression of the 1930s, when family income was substantially reduced, only to rise sharply during the economic expansion of the next two decades, when Boomers were just entering the job market. Today, many of the same similarities are in play but the results are far different.

After the housing and mortgage bubble burst in 2008, the economy made a slow but steady climb out of the recession, resulting by 2018 in the lowest unemployment in decades, inflation in check, and a bull market setting a new record for longevity. The stock market alone has added trillions of dollars to investors' portfolios, and employee pensions and 401k plans have expanded sharply.

Yet despite this economic rebound, many young adults today are struggling to make ends meet. They are living at home longer, marrying and having children at a later age, and putting off buying a home or other major purchases, all in an effort to try to get ahead of the debt they have accumulated.

A number of theories have been bounced around as to why today's young adults are confined to a treadmill when trying to reach financial independence. Stagnant take-home pay, student loans, high credit card debt, and less affordable housing play into the equation, but also critical are the cultural changes that have taken root in our society.

The Great Depression taught my family we could no longer rely on a job and income, so we adjusted our lifestyle and thinking in order to survive. Becoming self-sufficient and taking risks were traits passed down through the generations and instilled in each one of us.

Other families, however, decided safety and security were most important for surviving economic setbacks. Their objective was to shelter their offspring from the hardships they had faced by creating an environment that minimized risk and failure. "Better safe than sorry" replaced "Dare to be great" in these parents' vocabulary.

The "feel good" movement of today also is dominating the way people live and act. It used to be that everyone was equal at the start of a contest, but now they are equal at the finish line, when everyone receives a trophy just for participating, regardless of how much effort they choose to put into the contest. To lose equals failure, which many parents do not want their sons and daughters to experience. Educators are lowering test standards, many sports programs have eliminated keeping score, and helicopter moms and dads are quick to step in to settle disputes, rather than have their children do it. As a result, the young people are learning helplessness.

The government has also put up numerous roadblocks, making it more difficult for a person to take a risk when expanding an existing business or starting a new one. A litany of regulations must be met before the first customer enters the establishment. Although some regulations are necessary, the fact that hundreds must be complied with shows that most members of the Congress that make the laws have never run a company.

My stepdaughter was a victim of an honest mistake that almost shuttered her business before the doors even opened. She was in the process of starting a small restaurant in a western state and was working off a checklist of things that needed to be done. In part, she had to pass all food and safety issues, sign leases, buy the equipment and furnishings, secure loans, set up bookkeeping, purchase insurance, install all utilities, and hire and train a staff.

The check list was completed and the business was finally open. The restaurant flourished for a couple of weeks; everything was running smoothly until a state government official stopped by. During his compliance inspection, he discovered the establishment was not carrying Workers Compensation coverage. Although my stepdaughter quickly signed up for the program, it did not stop the state from leveling a five-figure fine along with putting the restaurant on its watch list.

Not only were all of the emergency funds depleted, but an employee, hearing about the lack of insurance coverage, decided to sue the owner, claiming she had hurt her back on the job and wanted restitution. The suit was eventually dropped because it was revealed that the plaintiff had used this tactic while working at other restaurants, but my stepdaughter still had to pay the court costs and attorney fees. The realities of owning her own business turned into a nightmare, and she took a loss when she sold out. The good news is that she was not discouraged by this failure. Instead, she was energized by it and went on to establish several other successful business ventures.

Many might view her first failure as an example of why risk should be avoided. They will opt for employment that provides a measure of security, good wages, and benefits. Although there is nothing wrong with this approach, history has taught us no job is secure, wages can be compromised, and benefits are controlled by the employer. "The more you make the more they take" is attributed to our tax system and why income alone will not get you above a certain level of personal wealth.

To advance beyond this threshold, a person must be willing to take measured risk. Investments, real estate, tax-free or deferred programs, and business ownership all offer incentives that allow you to keep more of your hard-earned money. Yet studies show that less than 50 percent of households have any outside investments, while 20 percent control more than 90 percent of the stock market. For millennials the statistics are even worse.

It is never too late to be in that 20 percent and to control your own destiny, but it will take time and discipline to educate yourself about where you want to put your money. The more you know about an investment or business venture before you become involved, the less you will be scared off by the risk factors, and you will build confidence in your decision making. Knowledge always trumps gambling when it comes to risk taking.

Introduction

In the 1780s, just after the formation of the United States, a Scottish professor published a disturbing set of papers. He said democracy was temporary in nature and could never last as a permanent form of government. He cited past great civilizations such as Athenian's and the Roman Empire that collapsed from within after only a few hundred years. The decline begins, he opined, when the masses discover they can vote themselves a generous monetary gift from the public treasury. From that point on, the majority always votes for the candidate who promises the most benefits—until there is nothing left to dole out. The democracy collapses under the weight of a reckless fiscal policy. The frustrated and unhappy population in most cases turns to a dictatorship.

The Scottish professor outlined the sequence of events that leads to the collapse. First the population moves from bondage to spiritual faith, from faith to great courage, and from great courage to seeking liberty. Liberty then leads to abundance. However, abundance is followed by complacency, followed by apathy. Then comes dependency, which takes the population back into bondage.

Today, many believe the United States is now situated somewhere between complacency and apathy, while others contend that with more than 40 percent of the population receiving some form of government assistance, our country is sliding into the dependency phase. There may be several ways to slow down or even reverse the process, but the culture in the United States will have to change before this happens.

This book is about risk taking, innovation, and a pioneer spirit, which sadly is being replaced in our country by a culture seeking security and guarantees, with a "what is in it for me?" attitude, especially among the younger generations. Social media has made people mentally lazy; they are more likely to accept what is presented rather than challenge the content. Young adults prefer interacting with others through texting or some other form of electronic communication rather than engage in face-to-face conversations. They see it as a way to avoid stress and to live in a safe, risk-free environment. The more isolated they become, the more dependent they are on others for their existence.

I believe a person is not alive unless he or she has experienced meeting a challenge head-on, overcome fears and apprehensions, or enjoyed the satisfaction of handling a risk, regardless of the outcome. This book will take you on some of these adventures, and possibly guide you away from your cocoon so you may enjoy a more rewarding life, and perhaps reverse the direction in which the country appears to be heading.

Throughout my life, I have encountered various degrees of risk that I embraced rather than avoided, which in turn has helped me formulate a successful business enterprise. Life always involves some degree of risk: changing jobs; putting money into an investment; or making a commitment. What is it that allows some people to survive countless perils unscathed while others succumb to life's lottery? Is it fate, bad timing, or an unforeseen force?

Risk is generally associated with putting ourselves in danger, often physical, but risk is also part of running a business. In business, risks include limited capital, fear of failure, lack of preparedness, and poor judgment. But these are just a few of the many factors that can turn a profitable operation into a casualty if the understanding of risk is not part of the equation.

As I grew up, I had my fair shares of accidents, some of which could have been avoided. It was not planned that the handle of a fondue pot would break, spilling hot oil on my feet, causing third- degree burns. It was unexpected when a stubborn nail caused a hammer to shoot back, embedding its claws right between my eyes. In contrast, rolling onto the blade of my knife during a camp out, or sustaining a severe body rash as a result of running through the smoke from a pile of burning poison sumac would be classified as accidents waiting to happen, the risks of which hadn't been assessed.

There are occasions when we have little control over our well-being, but we can still minimize the risk. I have lived through hurricanes, tornadoes, prairie fires, and blizzards, which would be termed acts of nature, but where others would seek shelter, I ventured outdoors to embrace the elements and danger. Whether it was foolhardy, poor judgment, or an adrenaline rush, my curiosity would put me in harm's way, when peril otherwise could have been avoided.

I have witnessed two hurricanes, one in Texas where I was stationed with the Air Force, and the other as a preteen in New Jersey. I had no choice during my military service because I was ordered to search for downed wires and to dispatch lethal reptiles that were washed out of their burrows during the peak of the storm. In the New Jersey hurricane, however, my brother and I took to the outdoors as the eye was passing overhead. The brief calm lasted just long enough for us to be some distance from home when the winds returned. Dodging flying debris, falling trees, and sparking electrical lines, we made it back to anxious parents who thought we had gone to visit the next-door neighbors.

I was driving back to Columbus, Ohio, from a business trip to Dayton when a series of tornadoes broke out, one of which claimed dozens of lives in the nearby town of Xenia. After the storm passed, witnesses described the town as looking like a World War II battlefield. In the distance, I had seen a funnel touch down several times before retreating back into the clouds. I was interested to see what damage the twister had caused, so I steered my car in the direction of the last ground contact. Outside of a few leveled year-old rows of corn, there appeared to be little destruction, when suddenly the sky turned dark again and the winds picked up. Almost directly above me I saw the unmistakable shape of a funnel cloud developing, so I made a hasty exit down the road. Looking back, I never saw the tornado touch down, but corn stalks were flying in every direction, and my curiosity quickly abated as I reached the main highway and retreated toward home.

A few years ago, I was helping some friends move their belongings back to Ohio from the West Coast in a large rental truck when I met up with a challenging situation in Wyoming. The interstate I was traveling had a series of gates located near the exits to numerous small villages. During the winter, when blizzard conditions make the roads impassable, the gates are used to shut down traffic and direct drivers into the towns for fuel and lodging. In the summer, however, motorists tend to ignore gate closures, assuming an accident has temporarily halted traffic for a short time.

That was my thought, too, as I drove the truck around the barrier outside the town of Rock Springs. Although traffic was sparse, the road appeared to be unobstructed except for a mist developing in the distance. However, visibility became an issue the farther down the road I traveled, and I discovered what appeared at first to be fog was actually acidic smoke that was quickly engulfing the cab of my truck.

Through the haze I could see a large grass fire that had spread to both sides of the road, forming a gantlet along the highway. With the smoke closing in, I slowed the truck to a crawl, not knowing what might be blocking the road ahead. The heat from the flames was becoming intense, and the truck's broken air conditioner only added to the misery. My fears at the time were not that the truck could stall out or the gas tank would explode, but rather the effect the searing temperatures would have on the two cases of premium wine I was hauling back to Columbus from a quick trip to the Napa Valley.

Part of the asphalt was catching fire, and though I was concerned that the truck's tires would explode, I decided to risk the unseen and stepped on the accelerator. I guided the truck to the center of the highway to avoid the flames and any vehicles that might have pulled onto the berm. As it turned out, I was the only one on the road, and within a few miles the fire was in my rear view mirror.

As I stopped to inspect my truck for damage, a contingent of emergency vehicles raced down the highway toward the inferno I had just left. Several of the drivers glanced in my direction, but I signaled I was okay and waved them on. I was afraid I'd get a citation for not heeding the closed road, so I felt it urgent to keep moving. Except for a few heat blisters on the truck's paint and the possibility of some overcooked wine, I was good to go and eager to get out of Wyoming.

These and other adventures have made for a challenging, and far from boring, existence. As you read these stories in this book, I hope they may cause you to reflect on adversities you have faced and how your actions—or lack thereof—might have altered the direction you have taken, especially when applied to business decisions and life itself.

At the end of each chapter, a business application reflects on a characteristic from the stories told. There have been numerous surveys identifying the traits that make up a successful business leader or entrepreneur, and out of the many mentioned, a dozen appeared on nearly everyone's list. These qualities provide yet another yardstick you can use to measure your climb to the top in whatever profession or vocation you pursue.

THE EARLY YEARS

1

As my twin brother and I grew up in the shadows of the Blue Ridge Mountains of Virginia, the outdoors was our natural playground. The Saturday matinees at the local theater had a great influence on our lives as we played out the stories from the movies in the adjacent woods. Westerns, World War II, and Tarzan movies were our favorites to portray in reenactment battles throughout the neighborhood. My twin, Richard, and I had an arsenal of weapons at our disposal, which we selected for use depending on the theme of the day.

If it was war, the slingshot and powerful fireworks were the weapons of choice. The neighborhood kids split into two groups, the enemy and the good guys, with cover provided by makeshift forts. Each side would use slingshots to lob cherry bombs and other explosive devices at the enemy. We packed mud balls around an M-80 with a lighted fuse and threw them like a grenade. Sometimes we encased small rocks in the mud to add a more lethal effect to the battle.

The next day a western scenario might be on tap, and bows and arrows would be the armament. We fought these battles in open fields where the grass was high. Each side would soak rags in a kerosene container and tie them around the arrows. We lit the rags, and the flaming arrows were launched at the opposing lines. The first team to retreat from the ensuing grass fire was deemed the loser.

Regardless of what role we were playing, the trusted Daisy BB gun was always at our side. The gun was modified to increase its potency by tightening up the springs and lubricating the barrel. The results were a painful sting to any exposed body part, so usually we wore a heavy coat during battle, even in the summer heat. It was fortunate no one lost an eye, although we all suffered wounds, and many nights were spent removing shot that was embedded under the skin.

My brother took our childhood war games to heart, and after college he enlisted in the Army and did his basic training at Fort Benning, Georgia. He then applied for and was accepted into the 3rd US Infantry Regiment, "The Old Guard," stationed in Washington, DC. Besides ceremonial functions and parades, The Old Guard was responsible for protecting the Tomb of the Unknown Soldier in Arlington National Cemetery. Richard participated in the Memorial Day wreath-laying with President John F. Kennedy and his wife, Jackie, along with other dignitaries. During the ceremony, the guard was instructed not to make eye contact with the President, so my brother concentrated on staring at a fixed object, Jackie's feet. He said they were the largest he had ever seen on a woman.

After the service, Richard moved west and eventually located in Colorado as a claims adjuster. However, his passion for the outdoors, along with hunting and fishing, occupied most of his time, and as a guide and writer he has traveled from Alaska to Central America in search of fish and game.

My brother's skills were honed by our dad, an avid sportsman who took us into the field at an early age. At first we were armed with .22 rifles, which were useless except for hunting squirrels, but later we upgraded to shotguns. The recoil of a shotgun left our shoulders throbbing, but we didn't want to have our guns confiscated by lodging a complaint. I solved the problem by not discharging my gun as often on hunts, thus giving sure-kills a chance to escape.

The thrill of hunting came to an end for me while I was stalking pheasants on a small farm in Michigan. As I walked along a thick hedgerow, I suddenly heard the click of the safety being released from a gun on the opposite side. I could not see the person on the other side, so I yelled to tell him I was in his line of fire. My warning fell on deaf ears. The hedgerow erupted in a series of rapid blasts, with tree limbs and leaves falling in all directions. I felt bird shot striking my leather coat and grazing my neck as I hit the ground. The firing stopped briefly and I could hear him reloading, so I stood up and fired a couple of rounds back in his direction. I aimed high enough to send him a message without causing any physical harm. I could hear the hunter beat a hasty retreat, but I never did see the idiot who was allowed to carry a gun. The leather coat was full of shot, but its thickness probably saved my life. However, I was not about to tempt fate again. I gave up the gun for the fishing pole.

In addition to hunting, my dad loved fishing, and it gave Richard and me a chance to get outdoors and spend some time with him. One of his favorite locations to fish was near the small town of Snowden, where a large dam crossed the James River in Virginia. The dam was several hundred yards long with a spillway dropping some 30 feet to the rocks below. In summer, the water flowing over the moss-covered ledge at the top of the dam was a couple of inches deep, but the only way to get to the best fishing spots was to cross over the narrow spillway. I always dreaded this part of the trip. It took skill to cross the dam barefooted without slipping or losing your balance. Being loaded down with a pole, bait bucket, tackle, and lunch made the trek a nightmare.

Each morning our small group would make the hazardous journey across the dam and repeat the trip in the evening. Dad called the experience "character building," but as an eight-year-old, I just hoped to survive the ordeal of each crossing.

During the high school years, Richard and I and a couple of our neighborhood friends would set aside a week toward the end of summer for a camping and fishing trip to Northern Michigan. Our destination would be one of the many famous trout streams that crisscross the state and eventually empty into the Great Lakes. On this particular trip we targeted the Manistee River, famous for the trout and salmon that migrated up from Lake Michigan.

To get close to the river, our car had to navigate a small fire trail for several miles through a pine grove until we reached a high bluff, where we pitched camp. A path led down the bluff to a section of the river that was over a hundred yards wide and quite shallow. The first couple of days were non-eventful as the river was running low and few trout were biting. On the third day, we decided to wade out to a small sandbar that separated the shallow from the deeper waters and try our luck. We all wore hip boots that kept us dry and gave us traction on the stony riverbed.

As we stood on the sandbar with our lines in the water, it didn't take long before our group started to catch fish. The activity was fast and furious and within 15 minutes we were close to reaching our limit. However, during all this excitement, I failed to take notice the river was rising and the sandbar was nearly submerged. As we learned later, six miles upstream the Manistee River Dam had opened its floodgates to lower the water levels. A horn had been sounded to warn fisherman downstream, but we didn't hear it.

By the time we realized what was happening, the water had become too swift and deep for us to wade back to shore. Our hip boots were now a liability, so we quickly took them off before they filled with water and pulled us under. Our vests and other apparel were next to go as we stripped down to give ourselves a fighting chance against the current. Both of our neighborhood friends were poor swimmers, so we decided my brother would go with them to the nearest shore, which was on the opposite side of the campsite. They would then hike the six miles upstream barefoot and in their underwear to the dam, where I would meet them with the car. We had to abandon most of our gear to the rushing waters, although I decided to hold onto the string of fish we had caught to salvage something from our trip. I waited until the three swimmers had safely reached the opposite shore and disappeared into the woods before I waded in.

The current was strong as I dragged the fish and myself toward the far shoreline. By the time I reached land, I had been swept nearly a mile downstream. Cold and exhausted, I hiked through the heavy brush, reaching the campsite as dusk was setting in. Hurriedly I took down the tent and threw all of the camping equipment into the car. I wanted to be able to follow my tire tracks back to the main road before darkness set in.

It was pitch black by the time I reached the dam, but there was no sign of my brother. The lack of daylight was probably a blessing since the dam was a popular tourist destination and three underwear-clad individuals walking across the spillway would certainly have raised the level of curiosity.

Cell phones had not yet been invented, so there was no way to communicate even if they had survived the river crossing but gotten lost in the pines. An hour passed before I saw what appeared to be three ghosts emerge from the woods and make their way toward the car. They were all cursing about the miserable trip they'd endured through the forest and the bad luck that had befallen them that day. Even showing them the fish I had salvaged did not change their mood. Cold, wet, and tired, they just wanted to point the car south and head home.

Ten miles down the road we passed through a small village looking for a place to eat, since breakfast had been our last meal. Everything was closed due to the late hour, and as we drove by a town hall with a bell tower, I heard shots fired. Wayne, one of the neighborhood kids, had rolled down the backseat window and was taking his frustration out by shooting the .22 rifle at the tower. We heard several loud clangs as the bullets struck the bells. I slammed on the brakes, grabbed the gun from Wayne, and threw it in the trunk.

A rifle was always part of our gear when we went camping in the wilds. It became a sort of security blanket, yet it would provide little protection should we run into a bear. Several years earlier I had been fishing at a private camp in Michigan's Upper Peninsula when a large black bear came onto the dock looking for the fish I had caught. Since my exit to shore was blocked, I took to the water hoping that the bear—even though bears are excellent swimmers—would not follow. Fortunately, the bear was more interested in the string of fish, and as I reached land, a camp counselor came on the scene with a handgun and fired several shots into the air. The bear gave up his quest and made a hasty retreat into the woods.

Now, leaving the village, we continued south on the deserted road when suddenly we came across a vehicle with emergency lights flashing. It blocked our path. As I pulled to a stop, a park patrol officer emerged from his jeep with a hand on his holster. He ordered us out of the car. As I would learn later, the tower bells were the village's warning system, and when activated they would signal approaching storms, fires, or other emergencies. When he heard the bells ringing, a resident had run outside just in time to get the make and model of our car as it passed by. A call to the ranger station set the roadblock in motion.

After we answered a few questions, the ranger ordered us to follow him back into the village, where we stopped in front of an old house with a "Justice of the Peace" sign in the yard. We were ushered inside a small living room, where a person I assumed was a magistrate had the television blaring. He turned off the set, placed a small American flag on a coffee table, and announced court was now in session.

My brother could not keep a straight face at the farce taking place. He laughed and was immediately issued a contempt of court citation. That's when we realized our small group was at the mercy of a sadistic judge running a kangaroo court.

The original complaint was discharging a firearm within city limits, but since there *were* no city limits, a trumped-up charge of poaching deer was the best they could come up with. We vehemently protested the charges, but our arguments were for naught. The judge had already rendered his verdict and was anxious to get back to his television show. The gun, most of our camping equipment, and what little cash we had were all confiscated under the guise of court costs. We left the house with only the car and the clothes on our backs.

The ranger who brought us to the judge was somewhat apologetic for the treatment we had received and said he would put us up for the remainder of the night in the small county jail. Since we had no other alternative, we took him up on the offer. The jail cell was small, with two bunk beds, a wash basin, and a chair. We took turns sharing the beds, but no one could sleep. Reflecting on the past 12 hours, we realized we had narrowly escaped drowning, had hiked six miles in the dark through a forest, and what we didn't lose to the river had been confiscated by a corrupt judge. Morning could not come fast enough.

Before leaving the cell, we were served breakfast, which turned out to be the fish we had caught the day before. Some legitimate inmates in the jail were also served the fish, so the town had probably saved a few bucks by not having to pay for a meal. As we were finishing up the first food we had eaten in 24 hours, a teacher who was touring the facilities with her students stopped in front of our cell and admonished her class to apply themselves or they would wind up like us.

Our car had a full tank of gas when we hit the road, and we suspected the ranger had paid for it out of his own pocket. It was still not enough to get us home, nor was there any money for food. Our group became scavengers as we targeted small gardens, cornfields, and orchards. A watch traded to a farmer for fuel got us the rest of the way.

Back home we relived the adventure with our parents, who were not too sympathetic, especially my dad because of the loss of his favorite rifle. He was also upset at how the justice of the peace rendered his verdict, confiscating our money and equipment in exchange for our release. My dad's call to our state senator set in motion a series of investigations that resulted in the judge's being relieved of his duties. As it turned out, we were not the only victims of his brand of punishment. A long list of complaints had been filed with the prosecutor's office for similar tactics used against hunters and fishermen who visited the area. The judge had developed a thriving business selling confiscated merchandise at auctions and flea markets around the state. Dad's rifle disappeared at one of those venues.

BUSINESS APPLICATION: RESPECT: (ARE YOU RESPECTED?)

For a business to be successful, not only should the CEO be held in high regard and esteem, but the people he associates himself with can also be a reflection on his character. On the surface, the Michigan judge had a title that might have lent a certain professionalism to a corporate board, but with his hidden agenda and corrupt nature, he would have become a liability that could ultimately destroy the company. Social standing and titles mean little if a person's integrity and reputation are flawed. When choosing a team to help guide your business, leave a person's "dignitary" status at the door and focus on his respectability.

When I launched my company in the 1970s, I did not want to sever my ties with the financial and banking industries since I had built up a strong alliance with many of the officers around Ohio and nearby states. Because of a non-compete clause with my former employer, marketing a similar product line would most likely put my company into litigation I couldn't afford.

While searching for an idea that would get me back into the banks, I stumbled across a small company in Georgia that was in a similar situation. The owner was having difficulty expanding his casualty agency, as many of his financial clients were starting to develop their own insurance departments.

At our first meeting, I was immediately impressed by the owner's unassuming demeanor and low-key approach. He had a strong Baptist upbringing, good ethics, and the people I talked with had nothing negative to say. In other words, he fit the definition of a southern gentleman. His wife, three sons, and daughter were equally gracious, and I was at ease with my potential new partner.

Financial institutions were never known for their marketing skills, and for years they became the punchline about opening an account and getting a "free toaster" or similar product. The problem was when another bank in town would promote, for example, a set of cookware, customers terminated their accounts and headed across the street to pick up the new giveaway. This revolving-door approach was not only expensive for the bank but also impeded growth and customer loyalty.

With our newly formed partnership, we saw an opening to address the problem, put money in the bank's coffers, and build retention with the customers. Because we were in the finance and insurance business, our companies dealt with intangible services that could replace the physical products being offered to the customers. Under the bank's group approach, such products as life, health, disability insurance, IRAs, and pension plans could be offered, portability was taken off the table, and the customer had to remain a loyal depositor to keep the coverage in effect. To make it more difficult to switch accounts, only one financial institution in each town would carry our products.

Each participating bank could offer one or two no-cost benefits to all customers who opened an account. But if we were giving away free services, who picked up the tab and how was money made? Our models showed that before we launched the program, approximately 5-10 percent of the participating customers would add to their coverage if it was offered to them. Neither the banks nor our companies had the time or manpower to interview each customer, so we turned to an annual open enrollment by mail to accomplish the task. The bank would provide a customer list, which we encrypted on our computers for privacy purposes before the mailings went out under the bank's letterhead. For convenience, checking account customers who signed up could have their additional premiums automatically deducted through ACH that would appear monthly on their statements.

Everyone was a winner. Because of the massive volume generated, the customer got valuable coverage at a fraction of the retail cost. The financial institution gained a competitive edge in the community, substantially reduced depositor turnover, and received 15 percent of all profits generated. From the revenue our companies received, we were able to pay for the customers' free insurance, cover our annual enrollment expenses, handle claims, and turn a respectable profit. Once a bank was on board, there was little service work to be done, as computers took over the program.

Our relationship worked as smoothly as the programs themselves for more than 30 years, until my associate's untimely passing. I doubted his integrity could be matched by the successors, so I exercised a buy-sell agreement and channeled my interest in other directions. At last report, his sons were running the daily operations with mixed results.

2
Wrong Side Of the Tracks

Lynchburg, Virginia, was the crossroads for numerous rail lines that came out of the mountains to the west and up from the Gulf States in the south. The lines made their way to Richmond and the East Coast or northward toward Washington, DC. Walking the tracks was a way of life, and they served as a shortcut to many destinations. I traveled the rail beds to school, along the James River for fishing trips, and occasionally downtown to see a movie.

Every so often my brother and I would try to hop a slow-moving freight train as it passed near our home, but we could never keep our balance running down the tracks and quickly gave up the chase. We were also deterred by a well-worn story of a transient who lost his grip trying to climb aboard such a train and had his hand severed underneath the wheels. Reportedly he was found wandering aimlessly and in shock along the tracks. What made the story so intriguing was the rumor that a large ruby ring was on a finger of the detached limb. No one ever found the hand, but that did not stop my brother and me from spending countless hours searching for this lost treasure.

The tracks that bisected our woods ran along a high embankment after emerging from a hillside tunnel. As far as tunnels go, it was not particularly long, although you couldn't see through from one end to the other. My parents placed the tunnel off-limits, but we used the entrance for shelter during rainstorms, and on each occurrence, my brother and I would venture farther into the mysterious darkness. We would wait until a train had passed before going in, assuming another freight would not be following too closely behind. Eventually we made the trek to what we called the "point of no return" in the middle of the hillside. Usually a train would sound a whistle when approaching the tunnel, which gave us time to exit if we were close to the entrance. However, the farther we ventured in, the harder it was to determine which direction the train was traveling when the horn sounded. We had a 50-50 chance of choosing the safe way out.

Richard and I were confronted with this dilemma while out in the woods with our dad. We had spent the better part of an afternoon looking without success for the perfect Christmas tree, and as darkness settled in, Dad decided to take a short cut home by way of the tunnel. Not comfortable with his decision, I suggested we wait until a train had passed through so as to lessen the odds of getting trapped inside. Dad was not deterred. We plunged into the tunnel's darkness and were nearly halfway to the opposite end when the silence was interrupted by the shrill whistle of an approaching train.

Not knowing which direction to run, our only option was to flatten ourselves against the tunnel wall and hold on for dear life. As the train approached, its lights illuminated the darkness, and we discovered there was slightly more room on the opposite side.

The noise was deafening as we made a mad dash in front of the locomotive to the other wall while trying to avoid tripping over the rails. Dad instructed us to grab onto anything that might be protruding from the wall because the vacuum created by a train in a tunnel could easily suck us under the wheels. The rock wall was wet and slippery as I flattened myself against it and held on as the engine roared by barely four feet away. The tunnel was shaking and the steam from the brakes burned my legs as I started to lose my grip.

Once the engine had passed, it became quieter as each freight car rumbled by, and I finally relaxed my hold, thinking the worst was behind us. However, hot sulfuric coal smoke from the locomotive filled the tunnel, making breathing almost impossible. Our eyes were burning and we pulled our coats over our noses, gasping for air as the caboose finally came into sight. Blackened with soot and making a hasty retreat from the tunnel, we emerged shaken but unscathed.

Stopping at a small stream, we took the time to clean up before resuming the trip home. No one spoke as each of us contemplated the fact that events could have turned out much differently. Upon reaching the house, my dad broke the silence by emphasizing the obvious: "Don't tell your mother."

A different set of tracks ran through a tunnel that passed directly under my elementary school and exited onto a long trestle that crossed over the James River some 100 feet below. The tunnel started south of the school property and became a favorite lunchtime and after-school hangout for testing a student's courage. A narrow ledge ran across the opening, and as part of the ritual, a candidate would have to stand in the center and wait for a train to pass directly underneath. As the engine approached, extreme vibrations rocked the ledge and thick, rancid smoke and heat rushed up from below. If you could survive the ordeal without exiting the ledge too quickly, you would move on to a more daunting task. Several girls in the school also took the challenge and their initiation into our small group made them the envy of the class. Most parents and the school were unaware of what was transpiring after the final bell had sounded, but in today's world the repercussions from the community over the fact that 10- and 11-year-old students were engaged in such bizarre behavior would make national headlines.

Surviving the ledge was a warm-up to the second phase of the challenge. The goal was to make it through the tunnel and across the bridge—a distance of nearly one-half mile—before a train arrived. Running through the tunnel was the easiest part of the journey. Crossing the trestle took time and patience. The railroad ties were anchored on each side by the tracks and a narrow strip of concrete, but there was nothing but open space to the river below between each cross support. You literally had to jump onto each tie to make it across.

The experience of being caught in a tunnel with my dad helped take some of the fear out of the unknown when it was my turn to run the rails. I waited until a fast-moving passenger train had huffed down the tracks before entering the dark abyss. Staying off the tracks and close to the wall, it wasn't long before I saw daylight and soon I emerged onto the trestle. Cautiously, I navigated each railroad tie and was nearly half-way across when I saw smoke rising up from the tree line at the far end of the bridge. Emerging onto the trestle was a slow-moving freight, blocking my escape route and forcing me to make some hard choices. I could take my chances in the tunnel, but I doubted I would be able to reach it in time. The only other option was to make my way to one of the small platforms that jutted out over the river below.

Approximately every 30 feet on the trestle was a small wooden outcropping wide enough to hold a single 55-gallon drum of sand used to extinguish brake fires on a train. The trick was to find a drum with little or no sand so I could climb in and wait out the passing locomotive.

As the freight raced toward me and I retreated toward the tunnel, I surveyed the contents of each barrel and finally found one that was nearly empty. Climbing in, I held on tight as the train approached. The drum started dancing on the wooden stage and I realized my weight was no substitute for the heavy sand that held the barrels in place. Except for a few boards that corralled the drum on three sides, I could have easily bounced off of the platform. Fortunately, most of the freight cars were empty, which lessened the vibration on the trestle; I was able to hang on in the barrel until the last car had passed. Climbing out, I noticed a number of the platforms were devoid of drums and wondered how many of them had met their demise at the bottom of the James, hopefully without any people inside.

I retraced my steps back through the tunnel, meeting a group of anxious classmates who had witnessed the freight train passing through. Although I had not crossed to the other side of the trestle, I was given a pass after telling them about my narrow escape in a barrel. It was mutually agreed upon that maybe we were testing fate a little too recklessly, and in the future we should curtail our initiation procedures. For once I was in complete agreement.

BUSINESS APPLICATION: CONFIDENCE (ARE YOU RISK AVERSE OR SELF-ASSURED?)

Every business must endure some degree of risk if it is to succeed. My adventures with the railroad, although reckless, helped formulate my approach to investing. To many, the stock market is just another form of gambling, where the risk overshadows the rewards. When you bet, the odds are stacked against you in favor of the house, but those same odds can be greatly reduced if you take the time to do your homework. For starters, you can get a sense as to whether a stock is fairly priced based on its high and low for the year and how the current P/E ratio compares in relation with the past and projected future.

Unfortunately, most investors want a quick way to riches; they rely on tips and hot stocks. They sell or buy at the wrong time. Human nature teaches us to hang onto our losers and sell the winners. For many people, the pain of loss is greater than the sense of satisfaction from a gain of equal value. To avoid investment paralysis, successful investors need all the tools at their disposal to make informed decisions when unloading securities that are negatively affecting the portfolio.

Several years ago I was approached by my in-laws about managing their small nest egg of assets, which consisted of a very conservative mixture of investments, including certificates of deposit and money market accounts. They had heard my investment techniques were yielding double-digit returns, so they wanted to roll over their portfolio into mine. My first and only question to them was, "How much can you afford to lose?" They exclaimed they could not afford to lose even one dollar of their nest egg. I explained to them that money is made by taking calculated risks and sometimes losses do happen. The picture I painted was outside their comfort zone, so they decided to stay put with their money. The fear of failure was greater to them than the joys of success.

I could have explained how their conservative portfolio was losing value because of taxes and inflation, but I figured they didn't need any more disturbing news. The actions of the parents, however, and how they lived also was reflected in their siblings, because most of them ended up taking secure, pay-every-two-week jobs with tenure that helped mitigate many of the risks in their lives.

Slightly Phobic

Among the most common phobias is the fear of spiders and snakes. My dislikes tend to gravitate toward arachnophobia; however, reptiles have always seemed to be part of my life no matter where I lived.

Virginia is one of the few states with the not-so-enviable distinction of being the domain of the four basic species of venomous snakes in North America: two types of rattlesnakes, copperheads, coral snakes, and my least favorite, the water moccasin. I encountered all four around my home in Lynchburg, and though the first three species try to avoid humans, the moccasin is aggressive and will not retreat if people get too close. Their habitat is near water or swampy areas, and they always seem to show up where I am fishing, boating, or swimming. I have had them drop from low-hanging branches into my boat—where they had to be dispatched with a paddle—or show up in the water when I was taking a dip.

My disdain for reptiles was further enhanced by an early traumatic experience. My mother occasionally hired a housekeeper to watch my brother and me while she went shopping and ran errands. As soon as my mother left the house, one woman in particular would take us down to the basement and lock the door. The cellar had no windows and except for a small sliver of light coming from the outside earthen crawl space, it was completely dark. The crawl space was the passageway for all types of varmints entering the basement in search of an easy meal. Where rats and mice congregated, so did the reptiles. On laundry day my mother refused to enter the basement until my dad had dispatched all the lurking creatures.

In this environment, my brother and I would sit huddled together, letting our imaginations run wild as we counted down the hours until our mother would return. The click of the door being unlocked signaled she was about to enter the house. After these experiences, I made sure that most of the homes I have lived in were devoid of a basement or lower level.

Copperheads were more numerous and also the least venomous of the four snake groupings. They were usually no more than three feet long, and their markings were tan and a reddish-brown. I have had several close calls with this snake, including retrieving a ball through a fence where my hand was inches from his coiled-up body. My dad was able to kill the snake before it could strike. A nest of copperheads lived under the porch of an old cabin we used for fishing trips; at night you could hear their movement around the floorboards. It wasn't unusual to open a cupboard door or walk out onto the porch and find a copperhead claiming its domain. At our home in Portsmouth, Ohio, the pet English springer spaniel took a strike on the nose from a copperhead while exploring under bushes next to the back patio. The bone plate on top of her nose prevented the fangs from injecting enough venom to kill the dog; however, her head doubled in size and for several days she was literately one sick puppy.

In Northern New Jersey, I was a member of the Boy Scouts and spent many weekends camping. At one site, there was a low stone wall that separated the troops from a dairy farm. On this particularly warm day, the wall was crawling with reptiles, including copperheads. Some of us hatched an idea to rid the wall of these snakes, then skin them and sell the decorative patterns for headbands, belts, and trophies, among other things. For the next couple of hours, the task was to dispatch the snakes by cutting off the heads, while not damaging their skins. We tossed the severed heads around the field as we peeled the snakes' skins from their bodies and placed them in the sun to dry. By the end of the day, at least two dozen reptiles had met their fate.

We had just finished cleaning up the kill zone when we heard a sharp cry from a camper walking through the field. Apparently he was barefoot and had stepped on one of the poisonous severed heads; a fang penetrated the sole of his foot. Enough venom was injected to cause painful swelling, which resulted in an emergency trip to the hospital. Under close supervision from a scoutmaster, we spent the rest of the day and well into the evening combing the area and retrieving the severed heads.

At another scout camp in New Jersey, we were housed in a series of cabins bordering a lake and a large spillway. The concrete surface below the dam was the home of numerous water snakes. While these snakes are nonvenomous, they can deliver a painful bite when provoked, and of course we liked to provoke them. Some of the reptiles were larger than my forearm in girth, and they would not back down from intruders who ventured below the dam to fish.

Our initiation plan for scouts new to the campsite involved these reptiles. Being around water, the snakes' main diet consisted of fish and other amphibians. When a busload of new campers arrived, we would string up our fishing poles and head to the top of the spillway. A few casts into the lake above the dam would quickly result in a fat bluegill, which we lowered to the waiting snakes below. The water snakes would quickly ingest the easy meal presented to them, hook and all, and then return to their sunbathing. Once the fish had been fully swallowed, the fisherman gave a sharp jerk to set the hook. The weight and muscles that came into play after the snake was hooked made it impossible to reel in, so we let the reptile back into its hole or crevice in the rocks.

Once the snake had disappeared from sight, but was still firmly on the line, we would call on an unsuspecting camper for help. We told the camper the fishing line had become snagged on the rocks below, and we asked him to go down and unhook it. The older scouts knew the drill, and a crowd gathered whenever a newbie ventured onto the spillway. The results were always the same. The camper would try to dislodge the hook by tugging on the fishing line or even reaching into the crevice. An instant later the snake would dart out of its lair and straight at the tormentor pulling on the line. The startled camper would fall backward into the water and be swept down the stream. He would emerge wet and terrified, to the cheers of his fellow campers lining the dam above. Seldom had anyone been bitten, as the snake's mouth was full of fish and hooks, but to an unwary camper this fact was of little comfort.

One of my closest calls with a venomous snake occurred while I was a counselor at a Boy Scout camp in the hills of southern Ohio. Back in the Sixties, timber rattlers and copperheads were quite numerous in that part of the state. Today, however, they are protected under the Endangered Species Act. During the dry summer months, the only water in the area was from the camp's swimming pool and a small stream nearby. At night, the ground came alive as snakes of all species made their way down the hillsides to consume the life-saving liquid. With flashlights in hand, campers would run the gantlet between the cabins and mess hall, always wary of what might be slithering underfoot.

On one such evening, as the sun was disappearing from the horizon, a scout rushed into the lodge to report that a rattlesnake had entered their overnight campsite about a mile up in the forest. Since I had rigged up a snake pole for just such an occasion, I decided to follow the reluctant scout back to the campsite. I had fashioned the pole with eyelets and a length of rawhide running through them to a loop on the end. The idea was to place the loop around the snake, pull tight and secure the head against the end of the pole. This would not injure the reptile and I could safely transport it to the camp's nature center and put it on display.

Darkness had set in as we arrived at the campsite, and the scene was one of bedlam. Young scouts were running around in panic, while others were content just to stir up the chaos. If there was a rattler in the camp, it was a miracle no one had been struck. The more likely scenario was that the reptile had been trampled in all the confusion. I yelled for everyone to shut up and to stand perfectly still. Once the noise had subsided, the only sounds we could hear were the insects in the surrounding forest. All was quiet for a few seconds before I picked up a faint buzzing sound, similar to a bee caught in a web or some grass. Moving my light in the direction of the noise, I saw a dark object barely three feet from where I was standing. It was a timber rattler coiled and ready to strike. Trying not to agitate the snake further, I guided the flashlight beam in a different direction while admonishing the campers to keep their cool. Usually I wore heavy boots when going into the bush, but that day, because of the urgency, I was clad in tennis shoes and shorts with my bare legs exposed.

My immediate concern was that a camper would do something foolish and cause the snake to strike, so in a low voice I put the fear of God into them about doing anything stupid. In what seemed an eternity, but in reality was only a few minutes, the buzzing stopped and the reptile began to uncoil. The snake was looking for a quick exit, and as it turned from me I went into action. I loosened the loop on the pole and tried to maneuver it over the snake's head as the rattler moved toward a group of scouts still frozen in place. The snake suddenly turned and struck at the pole as the vibration from his tail increased in tempo. Now the reptile was pissed off, and everyone who surrounded him became a target. Before he could collect himself for another strike, I slipped the rawhide noose over his triangular head and pulled tight. He fought to get free, as I lifted him from the ground and away from the campers. As far as timber rattlers go, he was not very big, measuring just over three feet and weighing around four pounds. No matter the size, his venom was potent and a strike would result in severe pain or death if proper medical procedures were not followed.

    I solicited one of the scouts to follow me back to base camp using his flashlight both to mark the trial and shine on the reptile I held in front of me. The snake finally stopped struggling and hung limp from the pole as we descended the trail. Concerned the cord might be too tight, I loosened it slightly and the snake came back to life. As we were nearing base camp, my torchbearer tripped, dropping the light and throwing the trail into complete darkness. Groping around in the pitch black he finally found the flashlight and turned it back on, only to discover the snake was no longer attached to the pole.

    I surmised that during the brief blackout the reptile fell out of the loop and we walked right over it on the trail. Retracing our steps, we spotted the rattler close to where the light was dropped. Its jaw had become unhinged from the struggles with the rawhide and thus it was unable to deliver a strike even having just been stepped on. Again I used the snake stick to secure our escape artist.

    Back in camp we placed the snake in a glass enclosure at the nature center. It became the star attraction, and during the final week of the camping season it was used as an enforcer at the swimming pool. The summer always ended with the camp being turned over to several agencies that sponsored underprivileged kids and delinquent teens. The counselors at the camp took on the role of prison guards as fights, thefts, and a complete lack of respect ruled the day. The swimming area was one of the favorites for this group and when it was time for the pool to close the kids would refuse to leave. The counselors' authority carried little weight and we were greatly outnumbered, so I would equal the odds by bringing the timber rattler into the equation. When the campers refused to get out of the water, the rattler was thrown in. Within seconds the pool had cleared and the snake was enjoying a leisurely swim by itself. We used this strategy often until a group of boys broke into the nature lodge one evening and threw stones at the glass cage until the rattler was dead.

I saved the snake's skin after the attack as a memento of a bygone era when camping in the wilds was a rite of passage that prepared a person to face the challenges life would throw at him.

BUSINESS APPLICATION: PASSION (DO YOU FOLLOW YOUR DREAMS?)

If you do not have great enthusiasm for what you are doing, chances are your business will suffer. In other words, passion breeds profits. As the comedian George Burns quoted, "I would rather be a failure at something I love than a success at something I hate."

As the first few chapters convey, I have always had a passion for nature, including serving as a park commissioner in central Ohio for a number of years. Being outdoors for me is one of the best ways to relieve stress and recharge the batteries.

Many of my best business idea have occurred while walking through a park or woodland, surrounded by the sights and solitude only nature can provide. In *Walden*, Henry David Thoreau referred to being alone as the time when the whole body becomes "one sense and can imbibe delight through every pore."

Unfortunately, today many youngsters would rather be sitting at home on the couch playing video games, making their virtual reality world an unrealistic substitute for what lies outside, thus missing out on life itself. They are stifling their ability to think, become creative, and adapt to their surroundings. They are living a fantasy existence.

People who have enjoyed a passion for a particular hobby, lifestyle, or vocation have often unintentionally turned their interest into a profitable business career. I followed a similar path with my interest in filming nature. I would usually carry a camera or video device when tramping through the woods, hoping to capture the perfect scenario that someday would grace the front cover of *National Geographic*. Though that never happened, my interest in filming led to a passion I had for the entertainment industry and movies in particular. As I grew up, Saturdays were set aside for movies, and often I could be found spending the entire afternoon in a darkened theater escaping into a fantasy world. I carried the passion of being associated with the movie industry into adulthood and was further hooked when several of my friends made it big in Hollywood.

Therefore, when the Disney Company came out with a series of limited partnerships in the early 1980s, I had no reservations in positioning my corporation to become involved. Disney was expanding its base away from making only G-rated films and into a package of 35 yet-to-be-produced motion pictures. The partnerships would provide the seed money in return for a percentage of any profits generated.

Investing in the film industry is not for the faint of heart as less than five percent of all movies made are ever seen. The risk is only compounded when the films' subject matter, actors and actresses, and distribution dates are all cloaked in secrecy. However, with the Disney brand behind the production, I felt the risk was minimized to a certain degree, which prompted me to get on board.

When the first few films that were produced turned out to be duds and quickly shelved, I started to have second thoughts about my investment. Rather than pull the plug and take my losses, I decided to ride out my commitment and was rewarded by being patient. The first big hit in the series was *Pretty Women*, starring Richard Gere and Julia Roberts, followed by several animated features including *The Little Mermaid* and *Beauty and the Beast*. At the end of the 35-film run, my company was rewarded with a substantial return on its investment, and I was eager to sign up for the next film offering. This did not happen, as future partnerships were canceled when the Disney crew decided to produce all future films without outside participants.

Some 20 years later, I took the knowledge I learned from investing with Disney and hooked up with a West Coast start-up company. Promoting a less ambitious agenda, we would use the Disney game plan and target high-net-worth investors who could tolerate the risk involved. Three full-length independent feature films with named stars would be produced to help mitigate any losses and assist with the marketing. To sweeten the offer, each participant would receive the return of their investment, plus 15 percent from any profits generated, before the production company took their share. Many investors were passionate about the big screen, so we decided to make them a part of the experience. Members were allowed on the sets for all filming, could mingle with the cast, be invited to the wrap-up and cast parties, have their names features in the movies' credits, and walk the red carpet at the films' premieres.

The first premiere was held at Planet Hollywood in Las Vegas. After the show, a Q & A with the cast members, followed by dinner and entertainment, rounded out the evening. Word of the event helped open the doors for new investors, and we felt this was the successful formula. However, the profit models for the film, and those that followed, did not meet with projections, so it was decided to pursue a different path.

Cost wise, making a film is the easy part, but profits are compromised in the distribution channels. Marketing can amount to upwards of 75 percent of a film's budget, with film trailers having no guarantee they ever will be shown on the big screen. Large production companies dictate what movies the theaters will show, and even if your film is approved, screen time may last only a week, with the owner taking a sizable cut in any profits.

Our company, along with many other smaller production groups, started bypassing the brick-and-mortar film houses and shifting our marketing emphasis to streaming movies through various outlets such as HBO and Netflix. Many of the expenses are recouped up front through paid subscriptions, pay-for-view, and other cost-saving measures. We can now make a trailer and show it on social media, asking viewers to bid on what price they would pay to watch the entire series. A high positive response will drive the price lower and get the series produced, whereas the project is scrapped with less cost if there is little interest.

Since viewers now have the ability to skip commercials, advertisers have switched tactics and are now strategically placing their products in scenes throughout the movie. This, along with targeting Influencers who can guide their followers to watch a particular film, has opened the door to additional revenue streams that can only help firm up the bottom line.

The jury is still out on how successfully this platform model will resonate with the film buffs of today, but taking the risk and chasing my passion—regardless of the outcome—serves as my own reward.

GROWING UP ... SORT OF

4
Lessons Learned

Beginning with elementary school, my learning experiences went far beyond the three R's. What most people would consider reckless I viewed as a challenge. I found studying to be somewhat boring, so to survive and help make the school year go faster I created a number of diversions both in and outside the classroom. For example, in Virginia my brother and I walked several miles to school, and as part of our daily ritual we took a short cut through a farmer's field to torment his prize bull. Our objective was to make it to the fence at the far end of the pasture before the charging bull could catch up. This activity went on for several months until the bull got tired of the chase and would watch us run—and finally walk—through his domain.

I also took part in other not-so-well-thought-out adventures. For example, one day as I ate lunch in the school cafeteria, I accepted a dare and proceeded to stick a metal fork into an electrical outlet. Sparks and smoke erupted from the outlet and the lunchroom turned dark. My actions had tripped the circuit breakers, and because backup generators were not yet in vogue, classes had to be dismissed early. As for me, I got a shock that left my arm aching and pretty much dead weight for several days, and I was also treated to a reprimand from the school principal and my parents.

My curiosity and adventuresome nature followed me into middle school, where science experiments took on a new meaning. For example, nearly every kid in the country is required to make an "erupting" volcano sometime during their school life. A small container is inserted within the volcano's cone to collect baking soda, seltzer water, and red food coloring. When the ingredients are mixed, they pour out of the volcano and run down the sides, simulating lava during an eruption.

I planned to make my volcano more authentic, so I added lighter fluid to the mix and lit a match just before the eruption. The ensuing fire destroyed my volcano. It also shut down the classroom, and any hope I had of getting a passing grade for my project literally went up in smoke.

Yet another experiment that went wrong involved a water-filled test tube, a cork, and a Bunsen burner. The project was to demonstrate steam's power to propel objects. When heating the water in the tube, the pressure the steam created would send the cork flying. I figured by allowing more pressure to build, the cork would travel farther, so I wedged it tighter into the glass tube. The ensuing results were a shattered test tube, hot water and glass penetrating my hand, and an emergency trip to the school nurse.

In high school, the chemistry lab should have been placed off-limits for most of the students. From the readily available compounds, a group of us experimented with and finally made a small amount of nitroglycerin. To test its powers, we filled an eyedropper and took the mixture to a third-floor window overlooking the school entrance. Dispensing one drop at a time, we created miniature explosions and pockmarked the sidewalk below. Thankfully, I was not present when one of the drops landed on a teacher, burning her shoulder, which in turn led to the expulsion of several students.

Another serious incident took place when someone placed a chemical mixture that exploded upon contact with water into one of the school's drinking fountains. Disaster was averted when a teacher emptied her coffee into the fountain before anyone had taken a drink.

The challenges of the past were just a prelude to what was ahead for me in college. My first brush with higher education was at a small liberal arts school named after a town located in central Michigan.

Among the many activities I participated in during my freshman year was to join a fraternity. One of the fraternity pledges was a young chap with the nickname "Elvis," who dressed, talked, and acted just like the King. He held a part-time job in the power plant that supplied the college with its utilities. He described to a group of us how the campus was served by a maze of underground tunnels that carried heat to the dorms and other buildings. The tunnels could be accessed through several manholes, the main one located between the campus library and gymnasium. Elvis implied we could easily gain entrance to the main women's dormitory, which was otherwise sealed like a fortress after 10 o'clock on weekday nights. We were intrigued by the idea that we could breach this tightly secured facility and maybe create a little mayhem.

During the winter months, the tunnels were constantly heated, so they were impossible to navigate because of the high temperatures. As spring arrived and the air became warmer, however, the heat was turned on for about 15 minutes each hour. That would give us 45 minutes to travel the half-mile from the library to the girls' dorm and back. The trick was knowing when the furnaces would come on, and Elvis possessed that knowledge. In addition, he provided us with a rough drawing of the tunnels' layout, highlighting the one we should use. In case the furnace turned on too early, our backup plan was to hunker down in the basement of the dorm until the next heating cycle began. However, this maneuver would increase the odds of being discovered and, if caught, probably being expelled.

On a balmy April evening we set the plan into motion. The library was now closed and the campus was devoid of people as we removed the steel grate and descended the metal ladder into the darkness below. The heating cycle had just been completed and warm air surrounded the four of us as we climbed down. As expected, the floor of the tunnel was dry, and our flashlights revealed it was larger than what the map had diagrammed. We were able to walk bent over rather than having to crawl, saving us valuable time in reaching our objective. Moving through the tunnel, we encountered numerous side exits that led to other structures around campus. As we approached the women's dorm, the passageway became smaller and more confusing because several feeder tunnels of similar size branched off the main channel. We spent the last 50 yards on our stomachs as we inched toward the Promised Land.

We emerged into a dimly lit room, which we assumed correctly was part of the basement under the dorm. Mechanical equipment and cases of canned goods lined one side of the wall. Sheet metal vents protruded from the ceiling and found their way to different sections of the heating tunnel. Each vent had numerals scrawled on it, indicating which rooms were heated by which vents. We discovered that by putting an ear to a vent, we could clearly hear the conversation coming from those rooms, even though they might be two or three stories above the basement.

We had accidentally discovered a new purpose for our exploration. Gathering information on private conversations would certainly be of interest and value to fraternity brothers who were dating girls in this dorm. We could easily crosscheck the room numbers with the people occupying the room, and although we could not identify each individual speaking, the general conversation itself was more than enough ammunition. Learning about the likes and dislikes the girls had about certain fraternity brothers was a goldmine of information that could be shared or sold.

We gathered a few good tidbits of gossip before realizing time was running out to exit the tunnel. On the way back we were confronted by the same maze of feeder tunnels, and our group became disoriented. As we debated on which path to follow, the temperature got warmer and our watches told us the generators were kicking in. We couldn't go back to the library entrance since it was closest to the power plant where the heat was generated, so we opted for a side exit. The confinement in the narrow passageway and the increasing heat made it difficult to function. Panic was taking hold when suddenly a ladder appeared in front of us.

I was the first one to climb up but found it difficult to remove the manhole cover while balancing on the ladder's metal rungs. Using my shoulder, I finally was able to move the cover up and slide it to the side as cool night air rushed in. As I stuck my head out and tried adjusting my eyes to the darkness, I heard a familiar sound heading in my direction. I ducked back inside the steel grate just as a large truck passed over the manhole where my head had been a split-second before. The force of the tires hitting the opening sent an ear-piercing shock wave throughout the tunnel, as we came to grips with the fact that our escape route terminated in the middle of one of the town's busiest highways. Dodging oncoming traffic, we were able to extract ourselves from the manhole and retrieve the grate, which had been carried several hundred feet down the road. We made it back to the fraternity house and spent the rest of the evening reliving our adventure with a somewhat skeptical group of brothers.

My explorations with the heating tunnels were over; however, several other groups carried on the quest with various degrees of success. It all ended about a month later when one of the students using the room heating ducts to communicate with his girlfriend in her dorm was ratted out by the girl's roommate. All the details about the tunnels were exposed, and after a short investigation, the grates were sealed with special locks. Our exploits became legendary around campus, but an even more significant event was about to unfold that would cement my college reputation.

BUSINESS APPLICATION: ADAPTABILITY (CAN YOU ADJUST TO CHANGE?)

A relatively new phrase has been coined describing today's business climate: "the power of disruption." It means the pace of change is constantly accelerating. For example, when scientists first sequenced the human genome in the year 2003, it had required 13 years and a cost of $3 billion to complete. Today, sequencing can be completed in one day for $1 thousand.

Experts estimate that technological disruption alone will make more than a third of today's companies obsolete if they don't quickly adjust and embrace the changes taking place in their industries. Former Fortune 500 companies such as Blockbuster and Sears have fallen victim to the disruption wave. In many cases, the larger a business becomes, the harder it is for the executives to shift gears and adopt the changes thrust upon them. Whether being trapped in a maze of underground heating tunnels or updating your IT system, the consequences are dire if no immediate action is taken.

A college professor once pointed out to me my degree would be useful only for my first job interview and thereafter I would have to learn a new trade to survive. At the time, I made light of his prediction, but in hindsight he was spot on. Statistics show the average worker changes careers three times and jobs seven during their lifetimes, and the task you are doing today will be obsolete within five years. We only have to look at technology and the re-branding of cell phones, computers, and other inventions to bear out these facts. Throughout my working career, I had to adapt to a changing business environment to be successful and stay ahead of the curve. From the legal profession, financial planning, employee benefits, investing, and entrepreneurship, I thought each endeavor would be my life's calling, only to discover it was just a pit stop along the information highway. It is human nature to be uncomfortable with change, but if you do not embrace it, you and your company will get trampled by those who see change as an opportunity to fill a void. It is not the things you do in life you should regret. It's the things you don't do.

A recent study focused on the millennial generation and how their failure to adapt to changes in their lives may come at a high cost. Many set unrealistic goals and very high expectations in chasing perfection, and when they don't achieve them, they just give up. They become overly critical of themselves and others, and they question their self-worth. Social media adds to the comparison pressure when everyone else seems to have—and post—the perfect life. Perfectionism can breed anxiety, depression, or even darker thoughts.

Not every gymnast will make the Olympics. Not every MBA will become head of a Fortune 500 company, but for many millennials these are the only goals that count. They are not receiving the message that trying your hardest and doing your best is still okay, even if you fall short of your objectives. Rather than give up, they need to learn to adapt to the hand they were dealt and take pride in what they have accomplished. The alternative is a lost generation that would rather toss in the towel than accept some failures as part of their lives. But it's failure, not success, that's our best teacher.

In the Cross-Hairs

When I attended college in Michigan during the late Fifties, many of my friends' parents were well-known in a variety of professional endeavors including politics, medicine, and industry. Although all of them contributed to the school's legacy, one family in particular stood out from the rest.

A well-known union boss from Detroit, whom many saw as a celebrity and others as a gangster, had a daughter attending the college. She was a somewhat quiet, unassuming young woman who maintained good grades and belonged to several campus organizations, including a sorority adjacent to my fraternity house. I got to know her through numerous joint fraternity-sorority projects, classes, and occasional parties. The father's reputation was sometimes a burden to her, especially knowing that fraternity brothers would dare each other to ask her out, just for bragging rights.

Her dad had a small house on the south side of Detroit. The house sat on a busy street loaded with used car lots.

Reportedly he would sit on his front porch and wave to the cars passing by, and people assumed his status was no different than the average union wage earner's. They didn't know all of this was a ruse. His real home was a mansion on a lake north of the city. On a few occasions, his daughter invited a small group of friends to her dad's estate for a night of partying. The compound was surrounded by high walls and featured a large gate manned by several guards. I never saw her father on the grounds, but I heard his daughter got into trouble for bringing friends to this supposedly secret hideaway.

It was Parents Weekend when the legend came to life at the college. The fraternity house was abuzz about the prospects of this famous figure's visiting the campus. My room was on the second floor of the fraternity, across the parking lot from the sorority house, where the parents were to gather for the weekend events. Although the street on which the cars would be arriving was behind the house, my fraternity brother and I could get a decent view of those who were coming by leaning out our window.

For most of the morning, cars stopped in front of the sorority and disgorged parents who were excitedly met by their daughters. However, the object of our stakeout was a no-show. My roommate, George, concluded our target had either slipped into the sorority house from another entrance or canceled the visit. Just as we were about to call it a day, a long black limousine pulled up adjacent to the parking lot and two large men jumped out from the front seat. One of them rushed to hold open the passenger door while the other surveyed the surrounding landscape. A short, stocky, slightly-balding man wearing a dark suit and glasses emerged from the vehicle. Our patience and perseverance had paid off.

George and I pushed our bodies out of the small window as far as possible to gain a better view, but a large tree obscured our line of sight. Not to be discouraged, I seized upon the moment with an idea that turned out to be less than brilliant.

During the fall and winter months in Michigan, hunting was one of the favorite pastimes for most sports enthusiasts, so students were allowed the opportunity to bring their rifles and bows to campus for use on weekend excursions. Although I was not an avid hunter, having a gun with a powerful telescopic sight hanging on the wall in my room projected a macho image. Using the rifle's scope, I would have no problem zeroing in on the entourage.

Leaning out of the window with the rifle, I adjusted the scope and suddenly a larger-than-life figure appeared in the cross-hairs. The details were so magnified I could even identify the union button in his lapel. As I spied on the figures by the car, I had a satisfied feeling I was invading this powerful man's privacy and that he was totally unaware of my presence. My roommate, impatient to gain a view before the union boss disappeared into the sorority house, broke my trance and caused enough commotion for the men to look up toward the window.

Seeing the rifle, the driver quickly rushed the union leader back into the limousine as his guard ran toward the front of the fraternity house. Realizing the possible repercussions of our actions, George and I bolted from the window and threw the rifle onto the bed. Seconds later, the door flew open and in rushed two men who looked like extras in a *Godfather* movie. As we sat huddled by the bed, I was impressed they had found our room so quickly from the dozens they could have chosen. Neither man spoke but went straight to the rifle and opened the bolt. We were thankful there were no rounds in the chamber as they continued their scrutiny of the room. Finally satisfied, they headed for the door still keeping their silence although one muttered the word "stupid" as they exited.

For a while, neither of us dared look out the window, and when we did, the limousine was gone. Trying to gain some composure, we filled in the rest of the fraternity brothers on what had just occurred; some were not too happy at the thought this powerful union might seek some sort of reprisal. I broke off any contact I had with his daughter, not wanting her dad to know what sort of people she was hanging out with. Word of the incident spread around campus, but George and I kept a low profile so as not to draw attention to our total lapse of judgment.

The union celebrity, however, was not quite out of my family's life. During commencement, an overflow crowd was seated in the chapel's lower rooms, where a closed-circuit television would project the upstairs ceremonies. I was told later by a college administrator that several union officials thought the proceedings were being taped, and they insisted on a copy. They were not satisfied when informed there would be no taping, so the union leader had his men dismantle the equipment just to be sure. This action delayed the commencement program, to everyone's dismay except for his party. He took a seat in the main chapel directly in front of my parents, which upset my mother.

During the two-hour program, according to my dad, Mom would continue a barrage of derogatory remarks about the union and its leader in particular. Although her words were more than a whisper, the boss showed no reaction to her comments. It was clear, however, they had not gone unheard.

My dad was the manager of a variety store in southern Ohio, and a few months after graduation the union tried to organize the workers at his location. Although they eventually failed in their efforts, it was more than coincidence that out of the thousands of variety stores around the country, an obscure store in Ohio would be the target of a massive union organization campaign headed by its boss.

Another time a gun nearly got me in trouble occurred at a bank where my dad made his deposits. Jack, as he liked to be called, had many hobbies, including collecting coins. Working in retail gave him the chance to check for unusual coins in the cash register every evening. He was particularly interested in Indian head and zinc pennies, silver dollars, and any other rare or unique currency. He replaced any coins with his own money and kept his treasures in a large safety deposit box on the mezzanine floor of an old Portsmouth bank.

In reality, the value of his collection probably was not worth much more than the coins' face value, but whenever I made the trip to Portsmouth, he would take me to the bank and proudly show off his loot. I figured the real reason he asked me to go was to help him lift the overweight box to a nearby table. In addition to the coins, dad kept a loaded handgun in the box, which he felt would deter anyone who might try to rob him.

As more coins were added to the box, it became increasingly difficult to lift it out of the slip. Also, a buildup of rust had accumulated along the edges. The inevitable finally happened. As my dad and I struggled to remove the safety box, the bottom split open and hundreds of coins cascaded onto the marble floor. The loud crashing sound resonated throughout the bank as startled customers and employees became fixated on the commotion coming from the mezzanine.

While my dad was on his knees scooping up the coins, I went to retrieve the pistol, which fortunately had not discharged when it hit the ground. As the scene played out, I was standing over Dad in the bank, holding a gun, while he was crouched down filling a bag full of coins. At least, this was the vision the two armed guards witnessed when they rushed to the disturbance. Although their weapons were drawn, the surreal atmosphere made them pause momentarily, giving my dad and me a chance to explain the situation, in the course of which I slowly put down the gun.

After hearing our story and examining the box, the guards were satisfied a robbery was not taking place, although they admitted it was the most excitement they'd had in years. Later, my dad and I both joked about the incident. However, this unintentional act could just as easily have turned tragic if the guards had panicked over the sight of a drawn gun and fired. I can actually say in this scenario I was lucky to have dodged a bullet.

BUSINESS APPLICATION: COMMUNICATION: (DO OTHERS UNDERSTAND YOUR ACTIONS?)

I viewed the use of the guns as no more than innocent props playing out on a bigger stage, but in the eyes of others there was a totally different perspective as to their use. All the wrong signals were given both at the fraternity house and the bank, where a breakdown in communications as to my intent almost led to a tragic ending.

When running a business, the objectives we are trying to achieve may not be construed in the same light by our clients, employees, and investors, unless our communication is crystal clear. Managers make the mistake of assuming the people they are dealing with are on the same page when an assignment is handed out, only to find out later the end result bears little resemblance to the objectives. Misconceptions can come in many forms, but once a person has settled on a conclusion, the chances of his opinion changing are usually difficult at best.

An example of a misconception and poor communications resulting in the loss of a valuable client occurred during a training session with my sales manager. I was learning the marketing ropes in the credit and bond industry, and my boss wanted me to go with the manager on a call to a large account. The appointment was at 1:00 pm, so we had time for lunch and a little prep work before the meeting. After we ate, the manager lit up a large cigar as he reviewed with me the tactics he would use to close the case. His confidence was high, and I was looking forward to his presentation.

As we pulled into the client's parking lot, I pointed out to my manager that he reeked of cigar smoke and it might be a turnoff for our client, especially if he was a nonsmoker. He smiled and showed he had come prepared by producing a large bottle of mouthwash and taking a swig. We then proceeded into the building and informed the secretary in the front office about our appointment. She accepted our business cards and disappeared down a long hallway. A short time later she returned and handed back our cards, saying the president was too busy to see us.

Hearing the news, my sales manager probed for a reason, while showing embarrassment that one of his top accounts had rejected him. After we pleaded for an answer, the secretary reluctantly went back down the hall and returned in a few minutes with a note in her hand. The message from the president stated in part he just happened to be looking out of the window when he saw the manager drinking out of a bottle. He went on to say he did not tolerate alcohol on the premises, and if the sales manager was using booze as a confidence-builder to make a sale, he would not be doing any business with the company. No amount of explaining would change the client's mind and finally we packed up our presentation and left the building. We learned that visual as well as verbal impressions could produce lasting consequences for a business if clarity is not at the forefront.

Auto Immune

In the late Fifties and early Sixties, Detroit was the car mecca of the world. Every concept and muscle car was on display along the main drag strip running from downtown to Pontiac, Michigan, some 25 miles northwest. In the Greater Detroit area, the highways crossed each other at one-mile intervals and thus were called Mile Roads. Woodward Avenue was an eight-lane highway that bisected these roads with a light at each mile marker, making for a perfect race course. The highway was lined with drive-in restaurants, where on Friday and Saturday nights the street rod drivers hung out waiting for a challenge. Most of the action took place on the strip between the cities of Royal Oak and Birmingham, a five-mile stretch largely residential and less congested. A cluster of drive-ins anchored both ends, offering a front row seat to the show that had become a weekend ritual.

Having a driver's license was a must, and you achieved the rite of passage when you could navigate "The Avenue." My dad had a short temper and very little patience for my brother and me behind the wheel, so he assigned the driving lessons to my less-than-thrilled mother. She would take us to vacant parking lots and residential side streets to learn how to operate a stick-shift vehicle, but we never navigated a major thoroughfare. My mom was a nervous wreck whenever she took us out, so the confidence factor was missing from our driving lessons.

One day my mother turned the chore over to our next-door neighbor, who volunteered his services after witnessing the stress she was enduring. Louie was from Denmark, where kids learned to drive when they were 12, so in his view we were already four years behind the curve. Instead of heading toward the parking lots, Louie pointed me toward the ultimate challenge, Woodward Avenue. As I merged into the ongoing stream of traffic, Louie lit up a cigar and instructed me not to act like an "old woman" behind the wheel. For the next hour, Louie never said another word as he leaned back puffing on his stogie with his eyes half-shut. When we finally got home, he told my skeptical mother I was ready to take my driver's exam.

My first accident occurred during a drag race shortly after I received my license. I was sitting on Woodward Avenue in my parents' black 1955 Chevy, which looked faster than it was, waiting for the light to change, when a car pulled up next to me and started to rev its engine, which meant, of course, the other driver was challenging me to a drag race. Gunning the motor and with eyes fixed on the light, waiting for it to turn green, I didn't notice a small sports car that had pulled in front of me. When the light finally changed, I let out the clutch and instantly rode up on the trunk of the vehicle directly ahead. Metal on metal is never a good sound when driving. For an instant, I think both drivers had the same thought: "Where the hell did that other car come from?"

I put the Chevy in reverse and slowly backed off of the sports car, leaving a large indention on the trunk. Both of us got out to inspect the damage, and I noticed the driver did not appear old enough to drive legally. My car came through the collision with hardly a scratch; the other car took the brunt of the impact. The young driver was visibly shaken and incoherent, muttering something about the fact that he had taken the car without his dad's approval. I thought he might be injured so I tried to calm him down, while thoughts of lawsuits or worse cluttered my mind. Since both vehicles were blocking the busy intersection, I suggested moving them to an adjacent side street where we could exchange insurance information and wait for the police to arrive.

As I was about to get into my Chevy, I heard the sports car's engine come to life, and with tires squealing, it roared down Woodward, disappearing amid the traffic. Trying to comprehend what had just happened, I concluded that either the sports car was stolen or the driver panicked and took off for home. Without insurance information and with the other driver leaving the scene of an accident, I also decided to take off and not try to explain the situation should the police show up. For several weeks I checked the local paper to see if a notice for witnesses or the driver in the accident had been printed, but seeing none, I felt some relief. Drag racing and Woodward Avenue were put on hold for several months. I didn't want to chance another encounter with a certain sports car driver.

On my street, it seemed someone in each household worked for the Big Three automakers. On weekends the neighborhood took on the appearance of a dealer's showroom with all of the shiny new models sitting out in the driveways. The cars were off-limits for us teenagers, but when the parents went out, we would "borrow" them for a few hours. The Royal Oak community had a suburban group called the "Banshees," whose activities were a far cry from today's drug gangs, although some of our escapades were well-documented and occasionally boaderline illegal. A few of the members got into criminal mischief, which cast a shadow on the rest of us, but usually our role was limited to racing and a few harmless pranks. Sneaking into an outdoor movie with a car trunk crammed with passengers, or driving to a run-down section of town to purchase beer with fake identification were the extent of our endeavors.

The Banshees did receive a black eye when one of the members attempted to steal a small plane from the local airport and crashed it trying to get it airborne. In another incident, a mannequin was dropped at night from a railroad overpass in front of an oncoming car. A number of ketchup bottles inside the fully clothed dummy exploded on impact, covering the car in simulated blood. The shaken driver called the police, who traced the ketchup purchases to a local grocery store and from there to a Banshee member. Our group then realized being a Banshee was becoming more of a liability than a status symbol.

One of the neighborhood parents owned a used car lot and scrap yard where lots of junkers were always available. On the weekends we would go out for joy rides to see how much more damage we could inflict on a vehicle before it became inoperable. The car was taken off road through fields and similar obstacle courses with the purpose of hitting anything in our path, including small trees. With the lights off, it made for a challenging ride.

Speeding through a small farm field on one particular weekend, we were confronted by a large, dark object directly in front of us. The massive tree that came into view was more than the car could handle, but our driver, in an attempt to avoid a collision, swerved the car too quickly, rolling it into a ditch. The motor died as we were suspended upside down in the turned-over vehicle. In the dark, with bodies on top of each other, we became disoriented and couldn't figure out how to exit the car.

Gary, one of the passengers, had lost his glasses during the melee and was frantically searching for them when he did the unthinkable. Gasoline was running out of the upside-down car and fumes were quickly filling the air inside. In his haste to recover the eyewear, Gary took out a lighter and lit it. In the flickering flame I could see the open window, which would be our escape route, then quickly grabbed the lighter and extinguished its glow. Fearing a fire or explosion would occur at any moment, we rapidly crawled out through the window and ran from the car. Luck was on our side, as only a few minor scrapes and bruises were the result of our car-wrecking adventure.

Once things stabilized, we went back to the car, and with everyone pitching in, we were able to upright it. To our amazement, the engine turned over on the first try, and although the roof and body were badly damaged, the car could run, although at a slower pace. Returning to Woodward Avenue, we were nearly home when the smoking engine quit for the last time. Pushing the car onto a median next to a large tree, our small group sat down to figure out the next move. It wasn't long before several motorists stopped and asked if we were okay and stated the police and emergency squad had been summoned.

We suddenly realized why we were getting all of this attention. With a destroyed car up against a tree on a Woodward Avenue median strip and all of us sprawled out on the grass, the scene had the earmarks of a horrible crash. With no plausible explanation for what had occurred that evening, I removed the temporary plates so the car's ownership could not be traced, and we scattered for home before the authorities arrived.

The local papers made no mention about a wrecked and abandoned car on one of Michigan's busiest highways, but I suspect the police surveying the damage were baffled there were no victims or injuries to report. For all I know, the incident may still be on the police record books as one of the most mystifying cold cases.

Many universities discouraged bringing a car to campus, so students received only a limited number of parking passes handed out each year. Fortunately my fraternity had a large lot, so having a car was not an issue. Because the nearest major city was a two-hour drive away, transportation was usually restricted to dates and keg parties. The college had a religious affiliation, so the administration cracked down on drinking, especially for those under the age of 21. In Ohio the age was 18, but only for 3.2 beer, so on weekends there was a pilgrimage to the border towns of the Buckeye State. Closer to school, each fraternity had its own secret drinking retreat. Ours was an abandoned stone quarry just outside of the city limits.

The problem with the quarry was that there was only one entrance and exit, making it easy for the Highway Patrol to block our escape route. To counteract this flaw, a pledge always accompanied us on a drinking excursion to act as both a designated driver and lookout. High above the quarry floor, he had an unobstructed vista of the surrounding countryside and would sound the warning if any vehicle resembling a police car came into view.

The road leading to the quarry passed over a railroad crossing, where freight trains out of Detroit sometimes impeded our progress. With a car full of beer and underage passengers, we were exposed to any patrol car that might happen to come along while we waited for a long freight train to pass. It was imperative not to stop when a train was in sight, so many times the race was on to beat the locomotive to the crossing.

On one such occasion, I was driving with a group of fraternity brothers to the quarry when a State Highway Patrol trooper eyed us suspiciously from the side of the road. Loaded with contraband and not wanting to get pulled over, I eased up on the accelerator when in the distance I heard the unmistakable sound of a train whistle. I sped down the hill toward the crossing, where the signal lights were already flashing. I could see the approaching train and felt comfortable there was plenty of room to spare, but my fraternity brothers were in panic mode. They were yelling that the train was too close and we weren't going to make it, which only served to increase my adrenaline. By the time my car reached the tracks I was close enough to see the train's engineer flailing his arms as he laid on the whistle.

Passing over the crossing, I caught a glimpse of another locomotive coming from the opposite direction, one which was much closer than the train I had been trying to beat. Realizing my fraternity brothers had been focused on the train I had not seen, I knew they were justified in their panic. A split-second was the difference between survival and disaster as both trains roared past the intersection. After our near-death experience, everyone was quiet for a few minutes as we continued toward the quarry. Finally, one of the passengers asked if I had seen the other train, to which I hesitantly responded in the affirmative. Assuring everyone the situation was well under control, I continued the journey, but deep inside I was fighting nausea about what could have been. As usual, my guardian angel was working overtime.

BUSINESS APPLICATION: FIDELITY (CAN YOU BE COUNTED ON, EVEN UNDER STRESS?)

The definition of being morally responsible for one's actions was not always on display when it came to driving a car as a youth. However, I changed after receiving a few tickets and having several close friends be injured in serious accidents. I was a late bloomer when it came to having the ability to act independently and make decisions that didn't involve dire consequences, but my parents planted the seeds of change

Like many families who lived through the Great Depression, my parents were accountable for their own actions in order to survive. There were no government handouts such as food stamps, which my father would not have taken advantage of even if available. He always said that whatever the government gives you, they have already taken from you in the first place. So my dad took on the responsibility of putting food on the table by living off the land. Becoming self-reliant, we planted a vegetable garden, learned how to hunt and fish, and canned preserves to carry us through the winter months. By today's government standards, we would fall into their poverty category; however, we never considered ourselves poor because there was always food on the table and a roof over our heads.

My dad felt that to escape the grip of the Depression he had to do more than just live with the status quo. He was not making much income as the manager of a small variety store, but rather than tread water with a somewhat stagnant job, he decided to expand his knowledge into areas where he could make additional money and achieve a more stable life. He had a keen ability to locate the best deals, whether buying a car, securities, or a piece of real estate. Over time he turned his management duties into a secondary income while expanding a successful investment career.

Being responsible in the face of adversity was the legacy both parents molded in me and is the fabric for the successes and failures that have followed me through my business endeavors. If they had pursued a different path and accepted the circumstances handed to them, I am not sure the results would be anywhere close to the same.

7 Jobs From Hell

As I grew up, I had a variety of summer jobs. Not having a job was never an option in my household. I was a camp counselor at both private and Boy Scout organizations for several summers, but I also had my share of lousy employment. One summer I spent painting old farmhouses that were in various states of deterioration. As I painted the shutters on one such house, a swarm of wasps emerged from underneath the eaves. In my hasty retreat, I fell about 15 feet off the ladder and landed on my back. I had the wind knocked out of me and could not move for several minutes. The wasps did a number on my exposed skin.

The next day, with a swollen face and armed with a can of Raid, I returned to the house only to find that when I fell from the ladder, the green can of shutter paint spilled all over the white siding. After the cleanup and repainting, which lasted an extra week, the money I was to be paid for the job had all but disappeared.

Another summer job involved the removal and replacement of old batteries from cars and trucks at a Montgomery Ward Service Center. In the days before air conditioning, with car engines running in enclosed quarters, the garage was an inferno. Most of the batteries I worked on were so corroded it was almost impossible to loosen the cable bolts for removal. During the course of a day, the wrench constantly slipped and my knuckles were slammed into the engine block. Leaking battery acid would find its way onto my bleeding hands, creating intense pain. At night I would get temporary relief by soaking my hands in a solution of baking soda and Epsom salt. The next day brought more corrosion and banged-up knuckles, and this scenario continued for the rest of the summer.

Among my worst jobs was applying whitewash onto greenhouse windows. As the temperatures rose during the summer, plants in greenhouses needed more shade to survive. To create the shade, I used a mixture of whitewash and paint to coat the windows. This process required a long pole with a brush attached, a bucket of whitewash, and learning how to stay balanced as I worked. The metal ridge between greenhouses, which was my pathway when applying the wash, was barely six inches wide. The long pole helped somewhat in keeping me upright, but the heat and sun's glare from the reflecting glass took their toll. A number of workers during my shift became dizzy and disoriented from the glare, and occasionally one would lose his balance and crash through the greenhouse glass, landing on the floor below. Numerous cuts and bruises and the occasional broken bone were the result. I lost my balance a few times during that summer but did not fall. This was another job I decided never to apply for again. Although I did not realize it at the time, each one of these temporary jobs, no matter how menial, did contribute a wealth of knowledge that helped me learn to lay the foundation for a solid business enterprise.

Between finishing my senior year in college and starting law school in the fall, I spent the summer working at a stone quarry near Portsmouth in southern Ohio. My brother was the smart one; he did not have enough credits to graduate, so he went to summer school in northern Michigan, where he did more fishing than studying. I should have taken a cue from an old Biblical movie I saw in which a slave begs to be killed rather than sent to the stone quarries. High school and college football players, along with other athletes, sought out the quarry jobs as a means of staying in shape before their fall practices began. For me it was one of the few jobs available in an otherwise economically depressed area of the country.

On a hot early June morning, I drove to the quarry site near the small town of McDermott, Ohio. I was looking for a hole in the ground but instead found a weed-choked field where a few men and pieces of machinery were gathered. Most of the property was owned by a father/son team who had been mining the area for decades. The prize they were after was a unique type of sandstone available only in small pockets around Scioto County. Because it could withstand chemical spills, it was coveted for lab tabletops in hospitals, schools, and research centers.

As I approached the small group of men milling about and drinking coffee, I noticed many appeared to be older, with weathered faces and hunched-over posture. Only later did I learn most were in their 20s and 30s and that the rigors of the job had an aging effect. This should have been a clue as to what I was getting myself into. We were each issued a pair of work gloves, steel-toed boots, and a yellow hard hat. It was also suggested we wear goggles and a handkerchief as a mask to help keep out the constant dust that was a part of quarry life. Although there was a suction hose attached to each jackhammer to try to minimize this problem, the working conditions would never have met EPA and government safety standards, had they been in existence.

As the bulldozer roared to life, we gathered up our picks and shovels and waited until the thin layer of topsoil was removed and the rock beneath exposed. About three acres of land was excavated and the shovel team quickly removed the dirt that remained. The sandstone was a grayish tan and surprisingly smooth to the touch. By the end of the summer, this flat piece of ground would be transformed into an open pit several stories deep.

When the soil was removed, the next order of business was drilling a line of parallel holes deep into the rock's surface. Although no gaps were supposed to be between the holes, occasionally there was a thin layer of connecting rock that had to be cut away. This is where the jackhammers came into play. Each hammer weighed close to 100 pounds, with a handle on each side and an air compressor hose attached. In normal use, the vibration from the jack made it difficult to control; both hands and body were needed to operate it effectively.

I found out quickly why the more seasoned veterans on our crew did not participate in the rock cutting. Straddling the two holes, I positioned the hammer's bit on the narrow strip of stone and turned on the power. The machine jumped off the rock and into the adjoining hole, taking me with it. The handles were wide enough to stop the jack from disappearing into the void; however, to keep from having the hammer get stuck, I could not let go. My hands become the buffer between rock and the weight of a 100-pound machine. Since there was no room for maneuvering, the jack had to be lifted straight up, using primary arm strength rather than leveraging. Once the jack was retrieved—with aching hands and strained muscles—the whole process started over again, usually with the same results.

Once the jackhammer's job was done, the next task was to split the rock from its shelf. This procedure required a series of small holes be drilled in a straight line behind the larger ones. A metal spike was then placed in each drilling, and men carrying small sledgehammers walked the line taking a single swing at the oversized nails. This process continued until we heard a loud cracking sound from the ground below. The head of the sledge was not much wider than the spike it was hitting, so these men needed both skill and rhythmic timing as they walked down the line. If the spike was not hit squarely, pieces of metal flew like shrapnel out from the glancing blow, leaving both legs and limbs bloody from the impact.

After the sandstone was dislodged from its base, the massive rock had to be moved out of the quarry. Workers accomplished this using a crane equipped with cables and a pincer-like device attached at its end. Notches were chiseled into the stone, and both ends of the cable hooks were inserted into the indentations. The crane operator then tightened the cable until the hooks were fully secured to the sandstone. The crane pulled the block of sandstone straight up and out of the quarry, where it was loaded onto a waiting flatbed. The massive stone was then taken to a processing area where it was cut, treated, and prepared for shipment to waiting customers. One of the many hazards of the job was evident when the crane was operating in the quarry. It usually took several tries before the sandstone could be successfully lifted away from the edge, and in the process the hooks sometimes pulled out of the notches. When this happened, the taut cable lines went limp, allowing for the giant hooks to swing wildly around the quarry floor. Death could come quickly to non-vigilant workers, and I had my share of close mishaps dodging the flying steel.

The deeper the excavation, the more stifling the floor of the quarry became. On the surface, July temperatures in southern Ohio were in the mid-90s, but with closed-in walls reflecting off a white powder, no shade, and a lack of air circulation, we worked in an oven. We sweated out more water than we could drink, and dehydration and heat stroke were common. When the foreman posted an opening for a demolitions expert, I jumped at the chance to escape what I imagined hell to be like.

Of course, I had little knowledge about explosives or what demolition entailed, but since no one else applied for the position, I got the job by default. That should have been another clue. Dynamite was used in the quarries to remove large amounts of unusable stone and to help clear rubble. The process began by drilling a series of holes in the face of the quarry wall in which to place the explosives. A blasting cap was inserted into each stick of dynamite, with connecting wires that led to a detonator a safe distance away. The wires were wrapped around terminals on the detonator, and when I pushed the plunger down, an electrical charge set off the explosives. There could be over 100 sticks of dynamite used, and not all of them detonated. This situation compounded the risk of quarry work should a pick or jackhammer strike an unseen blasting cap in the rubble.

Dynamite is safe to handle as long as it doesn't become unstable due to age or environmental conditions. Sticks can be dropped or tossed around without any consequences, which usually occur when they are being set. However, there are ways to change this equation. The person preparing for detonation must first dig out a section in the top of the stick so the blasting cap can be inserted. This seemed easy enough as I prepared a series of explosives. I was halfway through when one of the seasoned veterans on the crew pointed out that using a metal nail as a digging device was not a smart idea. Friction caused by the nail could easily set off the charge; a wooden stick was a much safer alternative. I quickly replaced the nail to finish the task. Thanks to an observant worker, my on-the-job training did not turn into a disaster, and I realized I had a lot to learn about demolition.

The next near-mishap occurred with the blasting caps. The caps, made of copper and about the size of a large rifle shell with wires attached, looked innocent enough, but they packed the power of a small grenade. It was imperative to handle these with care because of their unstable properties and sensitivity to the elements. Again a worker gave me some lifesaving advice as I descended a metal ladder into the quarry with a handful of blasting caps. The caps were touching the ladder as I climbed down and the worker casually pointed out that his friend had lost a hand making the same mistake. Again friction was the culprit, with the caps being much more sensitive than the dynamite I was also carrying. Disaster was averted, and I wondered how long it would be before my luck ran out. Common sense was necessary, and I wasn't always applying it.

My first big demolition experience did not go according to plan. The holes were drilled, the charges set, and the area cleared for the large explosion. The workers gathered near a storage shed some distance from the quarry as I wrapped the final wires on the terminals of the detonation box. When the all-clear signal was given, I pushed down on the plunger. Nothing happened. Frustrated, I was ready to slam down the plunger a second time when suddenly a series of explosions erupted from the quarry. As the ground shook, I watched the smoke, dust, and rocks shoot up from the hole below and disappear into the bright morning sunlight. A wave of satisfaction swept over me, but it was short lived. As the smoke cleared, the debris from the explosion that had looked like harmless specs in the sky a second earlier was now returning to earth in the form of large boulders. Everyone ran for cover as the rocks rained down around us. Luckily, no one was injured, and the only casualties were the tool shed and a pickup truck, which both took direct hits.

After that experience, I learned the proper way to set explosive charges. Rather than placing them straight up in the drilled holes, I set the dynamite at an angle facing the opposite quarry wall. When the explosion took place, the rocks were hurled across the quarry, ricocheting from wall to wall—similar to making bank shots in pool. By the time the rocks reached the top of the quarry, their energy was spent and they fell harmlessly back inside.

Although the job application for a demolitions expert was posted the next day, again no one applied, so I was stuck with the position for the duration of the summer. There were no other major mishaps, but when I went back to school in the fall I was happy to shed my demolition title, knowing this was not going to be my future career. The experience, however, did make it easier for me to concentrate on my studies.

After law school, my first full-time employment was with an established Wall Street credit and bond rating service. I had a number of courses to complete before becoming a Certified Financial Analyst, so I spent nearly a year in the classroom and shadowing more experienced company representatives. Once I completed my studies, I was transferred to a satellite office in Cleveland, Ohio, where my job was to research the financial backgrounds of companies applying for better credit or bond ratings. With a higher rating, businesses were able to obtain more favorable bank lending rates, saving them substantial dollars. After interviews with the owners, reviewing balance sheets, checking court records for outstanding liens, and talking with suppliers about their paying habits, I would file a report and assign a rating.

It was a tremendous responsibility to come up with a fair and impartial review not only for the company seeking a better rating, but also for the lender trying to avoid bad debts. Like a score on a college exam, one simple assigned letter could make or break a business and possibly send them into bankruptcy. With each stroke of the pen, I made either friends or enemies with the accounts that were assigned for review, because they had to disclose everything to the SEC and their shareholders. The private and closely held businesses gave me the most trouble, especially if they had something to hide. Partially completing balance sheets, withholding suppliers' names, or being uncooperative during the interview were all red flags that more digging was necessary before a final report could be rendered. A blank rating was assigned on incomplete reports, indicating to a lender that a loan would be at their own risk. The most common question businesses asked me was why they had to disclose so much information about their company. My simple response was they didn't have to comply as long as they were not going to ask some institution to lend them money.

The downside to this type of job was that the caseload far exceeded the time I had for each review. If a company made me dig for every piece of information and it became a time-consuming process, I was forced to take a number of shortcuts, which usually resulted in a blank rating and made nobody happy. The attitude was, "Don't get it right. Just get it written," which indicated management was more interested in the number of reports produced each day rather than the quality of those reports.

Being the low man on the totem pole, I was assigned one of the least desirable territories, northeast Ohio, which consisted of the three B's: the snow belt, the rust belt, and the blue collars. In addition, a syndicate of unions out of Youngstown had a strong influence on how businesses operated in the area. Companies located along the borders of Pennsylvania and the Ohio River were not very friendly toward outsiders, especially if they were going to have a say about a business's future.

I should have done more research on why the previous company representative for the territory now mine had abruptly resigned from the position. After a few months of receiving threats, enduring angry outbursts, and in one case having a gun pointed at me, the mystery was over.

My approach in this hostile territory was not to make enemies, as word traveled fast in these close-knit communities. I tried to learn as much about the business as possible before scheduling an appointment, hoping to find some common ground to put the owner at ease. I would not push the issue if management refused to reveal classified information, although I would remind them that their line of credit or loan approval would be more difficult to obtain without it.

There were some bright spots along the way, as I became friends with several influential officers who ran banks and retail establishments along the "Eastern Front." One such person was an auto dealer who was well connected in the area and had a thriving business that, in turn, justified a favorable credit rating. The dealer had a big farm west of town, with a large cabin on an island with a man-made lake. The farm served as a training facility for many well-known boxers as they prepared for title fights around the country. I was at first curious as to what lured prominent athletes to this remote corner of Ohio for training, but the dealer eventually helped provide the answer.

Across the river in West Virginia was a race track, and when I came to town, that was our destination after business was concluded. I was always introduced to a number of the dealer's friends, but I was careful not to reveal my full name, occupation, or where I lived, being both cautious and a bit paranoid. The purpose for our frequent trips was not to bet on the ponies but to present a new car from the dealership as a prize to some lucky race fan. This scenario repeated itself every month, which seemed to be a very expensive promotion for his company. When I asked him why, he said it was the cost of doing business, which to me needed no more clarification, and we quickly changed the subject.

Near the race track was an unassuming tavern halfway up a steep hill, where my dealer friend liked to stop after his monthly obligation was done. I went with him only once and was relieved I was never asked again. The parking lot was full of cars, but the tacky, red velvet lounge inside was almost empty. The walls were decorated with oil paintings of many famous Hollywood actresses in various stages of undress, and I commented on their lifelike qualities. Whether true or not, the dealer told me they had all posed for the portraits to helped launch their careers. I was skeptical this local hangout in a small steel town could wield that much influence until I was ushered into a backroom and down a flight of stairs. In front of me was a crowded, smoke-filled room with slot machines and blackjack tables, a veritable Las Vegas mini-casino.

My dealer friend was warmly welcomed, but several of the local patrons looked me over suspiciously. My host quickly disappeared to the crap tables and I was left to fend for myself. One of the men, dressed in a tux, was a pit boss. He approached and queried me about where I was from. I mentioned Detroit, and since I had lived there for a few years, I was comfortable in describing the area. We talked about several of the sports teams and after a few minutes he returned to the tables. I played a little blackjack, but the stakes were high and the money did not last long. Fortunately my friend was having the same kind of luck at the crap tables, and we soon called it a night. While at the casino, my main concern was being caught up in a raid with the Feds hauling me off to jail, terminating my financial career.

I voiced my concerns to the dealer and he just laughed and said, "We are in the finger region of West Virginia, and as the finger symbolizes, people make their own rules and outside authorities pretty much stay on the sidelines." Living there is not for the faint of heart and I only started to relax when we crossed the bridge and the "Welcome to Ohio" sign came into view.

Another unexpected incident occurred when I stayed the night at a national motel chain outside Youngstown. I had spent the evening having dinner with some banker clients, and because I had a morning meeting, I turned in early. Around 2:00 in the morning I was awakened by a loud banging on my motel door. Looking through the peephole I could not see anyone, so I casually opened the door. Again, no one was outside, and thinking maybe an intoxicated person was trying to get into the wrong room, I started to shut the door just as two men emerged and forced their way into my room.

With guns drawn, they knocked me back onto the bed as additional men swarmed through the door. Although they were wearing sheriffs' uniforms, they did not identify themselves, display badges, or speak. While one trained a gun on me, the rest of the small posse proceeded to tear the room apart, including my suitcase. After my bedroom was completely dismantled, the men in uniform huddled out of earshot. They finally exited, saying only that someone would be watching my room for the rest of the night.

Now that sleep was out of the question, I tried to concentrate on completing several reports, but my mind kept drifting back to what had happened a few hours before. When morning finally arrived, I grabbed my belongings and slowly opened the door. The parking lot was empty, so I headed straight to the motel office to get some answers. The manager I talked with had just arrived on shift and indicated he was clueless about what had taken place the previous evening. Although I did not believe him, I was anxious to pay my bill and get out of the area.

When I returned home, the incident at the motel was still on my mind, and the more I thought about it, the angrier I became. I fired off a letter to the motel's corporate headquarters demanding some answers, and within a week I received a reply. As it was described to me, there had been a robbery at the front office, and the night clerk was severely beaten. Someone reported seeing a man running toward the back of the motel, so the responding officers made the assumption the suspect must be staying in one of the rooms. All rooms that were registered to a single adult male received the same rude awakening.

In my letter, I described the officers as being unprofessional, not following protocol, and jeopardizing my life. Rather than validating my viewpoint, the letter from the corporate office mocked my assertions and suggested I was not supportive of law enforcement. Their response almost triggered a lawsuit, but then I thought better of it, knowing the hearing would be held in Youngstown, where I still had to travel and maintain a low profile. I did, however, write the motel chain off my list of places to stay, and it wasn't until years later that they came back into my good graces.

Like many large corporations in the financial world, the company I worked for had different sets of rules depending on who their clients were. Certain businesses received preferential treatment because of their size or influence within the community. Some of these "too big to fail" corporations were the worst offenders when it came to paying their bills on time or maintaining an acceptable balance sheet. Yet they continued to receive a favorable credit or bond rating because of their name recognition.

I was assigned to write a report on a business that was well-known but lacked financial integrity. This company had branch locations throughout the country and used numerous subcontractors to do their development work. In part, they made money by using a pyramid system with the subs. The newly hired were paid first, but the developer would find some reason to delay payment for the more seasoned contractors. Eventually some would get paid, but usually not what they were owed, while others had to file liens and lawsuits. This never seemed to bother the company since it had deep pockets and could delay the proceedings until the plaintiffs would settle for a fraction of what they were owned or they simply ran out of money to pursue the case. In addition, there was always a large pool of contractors to draw from who felt they would be treated fairly by such a large and well-known establishment.

I was given the task of writing a report and assigning a rating for this developer. It did not take long to realize they belonged in junk bond status. Balance sheets lacked details, court records were filled with liens, and there was a long trail of subcontractors who lost everything and had to file bankruptcy because of their association with this company. Therefore, I assigned the rating they deserved when filing my report.

My preliminary report was sent up to management, who in turn quickly sent it back for revaluation. I documented my findings and sent the rating back upstairs, only to be summoned to the boardroom for a conference. In fact, the meeting was a reality check on how important clients were to be treated regardless of their track record, which flew in the face of everything I had been taught. The company I worked for could not lose in this scenario. By writing a favorable report, they would keep a satisfied client and continue the money stream. Later, however, if a big lender lost money on a loan having relied on my revised report, the company would shift the blame to me since I signed off on its authenticity. Because I refused to play the game, my career with this financial firm came to an abrupt end, and at last report the two culprits involved in my dismissal were still doing a robust business. Life was simpler when I was setting explosives in a southern Ohio quarry.

BUSINESS APPLICATION: INTEGRITY (DO YOUR ACTIONS MATCH YOUR VALUES?)

Avoid risking your reputation and integrity for a short-term fix that could evolve into long-term consequences. Once your honesty and trustworthiness have been compromised, you will be distrusted throughout your business career. I could have been a team player under the charade the bond company was operating, but that would go against the principles I was taught. If you cannot be trusted, it will act as an anchor, impeding any progress you are trying to make, whether it is in a business or any other type of relationship. The old Scottish song with its phrase "I'll take the high road" is a good metaphor to follow when trying to build a successful career.

Here's a case in point. Two young men started in business at opposite ends of the spectrum and through a chance meeting profited from mutual risk and mutual trust. One of the men was a friend I had known both in college and while serving in the National Guard. He was assigned to the intelligence branch of the military, where, as a visionary leader, he helped bring many of the antiquated regulations into the 21st century. He was also working on a concept that would forever change the retail environment.

His dad ran a small variety store on the west side of Columbus, Ohio. The store was a modest success, but the volume of inventory the business had to keep in stock was restricting growth. His inventive son wanted to expand his developing theory that specialty retailing was the wave of the future, so he convinced his dad to set him up with a loan. With the money in hand, my friend proceeded to design a women's boutique at an upscale shopping area in a Columbus suburb.

The planning for the grand opening was meticulous, with every dollar carefully spent on merchandise and store fixtures. As the target day approached, my friend realized a key component of the business was missing. He had forgotten to buy a cash register. All the funds had been spent, and with no equity line of credit available, an opening day disaster was staring him in the face.

Enter a young salesman who represented a large calculating company. He was making cold calls in the neighborhood and happened to go into the boutique. After hearing the owner's plight, he explained he didn't have the authority to lend such an expensive piece of equipment, but he wanted to help—and he had an idea. In the trunk of his car he carried an antique register he used as a prop in his sales presentations to show how far the industry had advanced. He offered my friend the use of the machine until the store could pay for a new register. The register was large but beautifully crafted in an ornate design of gold plate and brass, and it was also fully functional. It became a conversation piece that seemed to fit right into the store's decor. The opening went off without a hitch.

As the business flourished, he opened more stores, and the calculator salesman became part of the success story, since most of the new registers were channeled his way. Normally when a business becomes too large, it is customary for the supplier to take over the account from the original salesperson, but my friend made sure the one who saved his company always got a piece of the action. Both men went on to lead successful lives, and the antique register that helped start it all now sits in a glass enclosure as the centerpiece of the retailer's corporate headquarters.

In this instance, both parties took a risk on the other one, but because both were also honorable men concerned with the other's welfare, the "high road" resulted in success for both.

ADULT ADVENTURES

A Wing And A Prayer

When I served in the Ohio Air National Guard as member of the Air Force Reserve, I was always apprehensive about traveling in a machine I could not control myself. Whether they were military aircraft or commercial flights, I was never quite comfortable relying on someone else to be in charge of my safety. This phobia first surfaced when I flew on a C-119 to Texas in the early 1960s for basic training at Lackland Air Force Base.

Upon entering the aircraft, each recruit was issued a parachute with instructions to keep them close by in case the plane developed mechanical failure. We received no training in how to strap on the chute, where to jump from, or how hard and when to pull the rip cord. During the flight, several recruits actually pulled on the cord and the cabin exploded in a kaleidoscope of billowing silk. When told there were no more chutes available, these unfortunate reservists spent the remainder of the trip white-knuckled to their seats. Several times during the endless flight to Texas, one of the plane's engines stalled and an acrid smoke filled the cabin, or air turbulence sent the aircraft into a steep dive. Although we were in panic, the plane's crew remained remarkably calm. In retrospect, the antics put on by the pilot and crew members were designed to transform us from civilian to military life and therefore the dangers we thought we were facing became more imaginary than real.

After completing basic training, I was stationed with a refueling squadron at a former SAC Base near Wilmington, Ohio. Our mission was to refuel aircraft flying out of Newfoundland across the Atlantic or to the West Coast. Life at the base was fairly uneventful since, as a reservist, I was required to be there only part-time unless called to active duty. A buddy system was in place in case of a call-up; each group of airmen was assigned to contact each other and provide transportation to the base in times of an emergency. I was attending an Ohio State football game when such an announcement came over the PA system instructing certain units, including mine, to report to base. This was a period in our history when the Cold War was heating up, so being called to active duty was not unusual.

Many reservists had to travel much farther to base than the members of my buddy system, so I felt no sense of urgency and stayed until the game ended. By the time our carpool got together and we headed toward Wilmington, several hours had passed since the original announcement.

As we approached the base, we were stopped by Air Force police and told to return home to Columbus. It was not until several days later I learned about the plane crash that had closed the base. Apparently a C-119 out of Fort Campbell, Kentucky, had gone down, killing several airmen and enlisted personal. As fate would have it, our buddy system's delayed response to the emergency call-up probably kept us from joining the crew members on the ill-fated flight.

My closest brush with an air disaster occurred on a routine commercial flight from Columbus to Cleveland, Ohio, in the fall of 1963. The company I was working for held an annual sales meeting to kick off its yearly campaign, and I was representing the Columbus office. Lake Central Airlines based at Port Columbus (now John Glenn International Airport) specialized in shorter flights, using their fleet of aging Douglas DC-3s. These planes were converted C-47s that carried the workload for troops and supplies during the Second World War. Cruising speed for the DC-3s was around 200 miles per hour on a fixed-wing two-propeller frame. Passenger capacity was around 25, along with two crew and one flight attendant. There were two seats on one side of the plane and one on the other with an aisle so steep passengers would use the seats in front of them to help pull themselves up to the front of the aircraft.

I was in a single seat overlooking the wing as the plane taxied and became airborne. Although I had been on this type of aircraft before, this particular plane felt sluggish and seemed to labor in flight. I remember looking out the window at a large body of water and was told by the flight attendant we were crossing over Hoover Reservoir, just north of the airport. A few minutes later I viewed the same reservoir slowly passing under me and realized that our aircraft was nowhere near its normal cruising speed. By the time we reached the Akron-Canton Airport, it was already dark and we were nearly an hour behind our scheduled landing time. I asked the attendant about the delay and she said the aircraft was carrying a large shipment of mufflers and batteries and the weight was having some effect on the plane's air speed.

At the airport, a group of golfers from a PGA tour event in Akron boarded the plane for the short hop to Cleveland and connecting flights. I could only imagine what the added weight of the golfers, clubs, and luggage would have on the plane's performance. It didn't take long to find out.

The runways at Akron-Canton are shorter than at many major airports and drop off sharply at the end of the taxi area onto a major highway. Under normal conditions, the runway is more than adequate for a DC-3 and other prop planes, but with the additional payload it struggled to get airborne. No sooner did we clear the runway then I noticed smoke coming from the left engine. Other passengers also became aware of the engine problem and started an animated conversation with the flight attendant. The pilots also were taking notice of the flashing lights on their instrument panels, which the passengers also could see because there were no doors to the cockpit. Shortly, an announcement came over the intercom stating the aircraft was experiencing a minor technical issue, but we were assured the DC-3 could easily fly on one engine. A moment later the propeller on the smoking engine was shut down.

The anxiety in the cabin subsided as the plane continued its flight path to Cleveland. As the aircraft started its descent into Cleveland-Hopkins Airport, droplets of oil speckled the windows on the starboard side. The right engine was now in trouble, as an increasing film of oil obstructed the passengers' view. Far down below I could see flashing lights of emergency vehicles as the aircraft made a steep dive for the lighted runways. With little room for error, the pilot picked the closest landing strip, knowing the engine could stall at any second. The plane touched down in a billow of white foam, giving the impression we had landed on a cloud or the aircraft was going through a car wash. I could see fire engines following us down the runway as the plane labored toward the terminal. With less than one engine, however, the DC-3 did not have enough power to hold a straight line, and after making several attempts to stay on the tarmac, the captain shut down the aircraft. We disembarked from the cabin onto a surreal foam-covered runway about a quarter-mile from the terminal gates. Rather than wait for transportation, a group of us with carry-on luggage decided to hoof it through the foam to the gate and thus get as far away as possible from the still-smoking fuselage. Once inside the terminal, I did not stay around for the debriefing that usually accompanies such an event and instead went to the nearest ground transportation for the final leg of my journey to a downtown Cleveland hotel.

The flight back to Columbus, although anticlimactic, did have its moments. As the DC-3 started down the runway, a loud banging sound came from the rear door compartment. The plane braked hard as a flight attendant opened the rear hatch and yanked in the stairs that were still attached to the fuselage. A series of FAA investigations coupled with numerous financial difficulties were the demise of Lake Central; it was finally acquired by another airline and its fleet of DC-3s was taken out of active service.

BUSINESS APPLICATION: ACCOUNTABILITY (DO YOU ACCEPT RESPONSIBILITY FOR YOUR ACTIONS?)

As my flying experiences illustrate, sometimes you have to place your faith and confidence in others to take control, with the results not always being positive. Accountability sometimes has its drawbacks.

This was the case when, along with a small group of investors, I help developed a revolutionary approach to solving a troubling problem most hospitals across the nation were facing. Their balance sheets were top-heavy in receivables, with a high percentage past due, resulting in a negative effect on their bottom lines. The health care industry typically would not send out bills to their patients until the insurance companies had paid their portion of the claims, a procedure that sometimes took up to six months. By then, the patients assumed all bills had been paid and were not too pleased to receive invoices from the hospitals marked "past due." Many had not budgeted for the extra cost while others simply refused to pay.

Our program in part was designed to work with the patients and the insurance companies, determining far in advance what payments would be made to the hospitals and then setting up a plan for the clients to pay the balance. With the patients' share of the bill identified up front and designing a convenient way to settle the account, payments were more likely to be made in a timely manner, and the hospitals would be sending fewer claims to a collection agency.

Although, in one case, this concept received initial approval from the hospital administrators, the final test for acceptance had to come from the accounts receivable department, and this was where the trouble began. On the surface, the staff was enthusiastic about incorporating the program into their collection division, while at the same time they sought to sabotage its introduction. The fear of their department's authority being diminished and the possible loss of jobs was too big a risk for them to approve the program, even though it would benefit the hospital as a whole. In the end, the collection division at the hospital convinced management our programs were too risky to adopt and they stayed the course by continuing their antiquated ways of doing business. The administration dropped the ball by not being accountable regarding their patients' well-being.

A sales manager once told me that in marketing a product you must appeal to a person or company's need and greed. In this case, the hospitals definitely needed the program but the "what's in it for me?" factor was missing. Building a moat around your department and to shut out new ideas is one of the key reasons businesses fail. If you call on outside consultants to help launch your business, try to determine if they are visionaries who embrace new ideas or obstructionists who see only risk and pitfalls with every decision you make. Save your money on their services if their only objective is to point out everything that could go wrong.

Home Invasion

Close calls can happen anywhere, but our homes should be safe havens in which to retreat. Barring fires, tornadoes, or floods, the idea that our home is our castle should give some comfort in the protection it provides. Although natural disasters are usually uncontrollable, unexpected events of other types can leave us just as vulnerable as trying to survive a hurricane.

A number of years ago, my family and I bought our first home on a quiet street in a Columbus, Ohio, suburb. Along with several upgrades, we added a hot tub to a small enclosure off the back deck. The tub was used for parties and other social gatherings as well as enjoyment by the family. One rule in force was the tub could not be used by children unless a parent was present. Because of the dangers generated by the heat, a person could suffer a fainting spell and possibly drown if they remained in the water too long.

One weekend, as a friend of mine and another couple were heading out for dinner, I reminded my son, who was having a sleepover with several of his classmates, about the hot tub rule. When we returned later that night, I suggested a glass of wine and a dip in the tub to cap off the evening. Although the offer was intriguing to them, our friends decided to take a rain check and call it a night. The boys were still playing videos in the basement as I retired to the bedroom.

I awoke early, made a cup of coffee, and went out on the deck with the morning paper. As I sat there soaking up the new day, I happened to glance toward the small room and noticed that the hot tub cover had been moved.

Upon closer inspection, I also noticed water on the floor, which indicated the tub had been used the night before. Anger crept over me as I stood observing the scene, when suddenly I felt a tingling sensation in my feet. Looking down, I saw that my sweat socks were slowly dissolving and my exposed skin was turning red. This was not water on the floor, but acid. I shot into the house and put my feet in the only place where I could get relief, the toilet. After several flushes, the pain subsided and outside of a few small blisters and a reddish rash, my feet returned to normal, minus the dissolved socks.

I put on a pair of shoes and returned to the porch, trying to get a handle on what had just happened. The inside plastic liner of the tub was pitted and melted in several spots. and an acrid smell that irritated my nose and eyes, rose from the water. Someone had poured acid into the hot tub with the obvious intent to cause bodily harm.

I went to the top of the basement stairs and yelled for everyone to get up. I informed my son's guests about what I had discovered, but each boy stated he had no knowledge of the incident. I told them they had five minutes to get their stories together before I called the police and let them sort it out.

Finally, one of the neighborhood boys stepped forward to explain his involvement and motive for contaminating the waters. He said that pouring a large amount of sulfuric acid into the tub would dissolve the bathing suits of the girls they planned to call over for a dip. This boy was known to have a genius IQ, but he lacked the ability to comprehend the consequences of the actions he took. In fact, if I were a Secret Service agent observing a crowd of people, his various mannerisms would definitely catch my eye. Several other boys were also in on the plot, but my son said he went to bed early and was not aware of what was taking place, which also did not please me.

I had each boy call his parents to inform them of his role in the night's events, so no one was let off the hook. To avoid prosecution of his son, the perpetrator's father had to pay for all damages (including a new hot tub) and make sure that his boy received counseling. Since he was an attorney, I assume he understood the gravity of the matter, but just to make sure, I filed a police report and left the possibility of future prosecution on the table. The father also disclosed that a number of old batteries from which the acid was obtained were in his garage, but he assumed they were being used for a science project at his son's school.

The fact that no girls showed up at the house and our friends decided not to take the plunge the night before were blessings because no one became a victim of this deadly experiment. In either case, the heat would have masked the chemical burns until it was too late. Most of our bodies would have sustained third-degree burns with perhaps a fatal outcome.

Consequences for your actions can have a far-reaching effect both in life and in business. Several years after the hot tub incident, I was sitting on a foundation board that awarded full-ride international scholarships to the best and brightest students from the local universities. As you probably surmised, one of the applicants for the interview turned out to be the same boy who had sabotaged the tub. When he entered the room and saw I was one of the interviewers, he did an abrupt about-face and walked out. I might have cut him some slack and at least given him a chance to apply, but he could not escape his past, and he will possibly carry that guilt of the incident as a heavy weight throughout his life.

Another unexpected event occurred while my kids were away at school. I left the house on a cold but sunny early November day to cast my ballot at my local precinct. I was gone for about 30 minutes, and as I pulled into my driveway and opened the garage door I sensed something was not right. Sitting on my garage floor were several stereo speakers, wires, and other assorted junk. I exited the car, entered the house, and suddenly realized I had been the victim of a burglary. A quick assessment revealed that most of my kitchen appliances were gone, along with the television, stereo, and other electronic devices. I was fortunate that the house was not vandalized, with only minor damage done when the items were removed. The police felt the burglars were professional adults rather than teenagers because of the lack of destruction and the selection of goods taken. The thieves used metal detectors to go through my dresser and take pieces of jewelry that were hidden in my socks. Ice on the kitchen floor indicated they also had checked the freezer, where many homeowners stash their valuables.

The police estimated that it took no longer than 20 minutes for the robbers to enter and leave the premises. My house had probably been under surveillance, and when I left to go vote they pulled a van into the garage and put down the door using a universal remote. With the door shut, they could continue their work unimpeded.

It was fortunate I did not confront the thieves when I pulled into the driveway. My car would have blocked their escape route and since two of my loaded rifles were part of the stolen property, desperate men might have resorted to desperate measures. Also, the ice on the kitchen floor had not yet melted, which told me that crossing paths with the robbers was narrowed down to a matter of minutes.

The police and insurance company took an itemized list of the stolen property, but the reality of recovery was slim to none. What the burglars could not fence they would sell at a flea market in southern Ohio or West Virginia. It appeared from what the thieves took that they had a map of the rooms and a shopping list of items to grab, knowing exactly where everything was located. I concluded that a housekeeper I had let go several weeks earlier was the inside contact, using her familiarity with the premises and which items were located in which rooms. Her whereabouts, however, were unknown, as she left a bogus contact number upon dismissal.

I tested fate again when a partner and I bought a parcel of land northwest of Columbus. The property was 160 acres divided among cropland, some woods, and a large lake. Included were two old farmhouses, which each family would use as a weekend retreat once they were made livable. The short-term goal was to enjoy all of the amenities with our children and perhaps develop the land as an investment.

My partner lived several hours away, so he needed to make his home more livable for the weekend; my family was closer to the property, so I upgraded our farmhouse with the bare essentials. The property was located at the end of a deserted road to nowhere and thus became the target of vandals. Posted signs, gated driveways, and sheriff patrols did little to curb the destruction we faced each weekend. Even a canoe I had purchased the week before and chained to a large tree was stolen, with the thieves cutting down the tree to remove the chain. My partner and I finally decided our families would share one of the houses and rent the other so we would have security of someone living 24/7 on the property.

The larger of the two farmhouses was rented to a family with a young child; the couple had grown up in the area, and we were willing to charge less rent in exchange for their keeping up the property and taking care of minor repairs. The father had spent some time in the military and lived the part by dressing in army fatigues and occasionally wearing camouflage face paint. He was usually seen carrying a crossbow or another form of weaponry, which I figured would be a good deterrent against trespassers.

Things went well for the first few months, with fewer incidents occurring from the outsiders. We never knew exactly what the father of the rental family did for a living, but he was gone for extended periods of time, leaving his wife and child alone on the homestead. His prolonged absences also began to show in the lack of upkeep around the premises, which was a violation of our rental agreement. His wife could offer little clue as to his whereabouts, but she was visibly stressed about his disappearance. By now, the rent money was only trickling in each month, and one day it stopped altogether. The wife and child had little food in the house, and on several occasions we took them meals to tide them over for another day.

My partner and I finally bit the bullet and sent out an eviction notice, followed up by a visit from the local sheriff. The father was still a no-show and I felt sorry for putting his poor wife through the legal hassle. On my next visit to the farm, the house was vacant. Reportedly she and the child had moved in with her parents.

Not to my surprise, as I entered the vacated house I was confronted by piles of trash, graffiti on the walls, and broken fixtures. The basement door was left open and glass from the light bulbs littered the floor. Retrieving a flashlight, I started down the stairs and found that part of the cellar floor was flooded. As I stood on the steps following the beam of my flashlight, I happened to look down and noticed a thin, taut wire stretched across the stairwell. One end of the wire was attached to a nail protruding from the wall, while the other end was tied to an object wedged between the railing supports. Upon closer inspection, I became aware that a booby trap had been set, with the wire wrapped around the pin of an explosive device.

I wondered what other surprises were waiting for me in the darkness. The basement was empty except for several water-soaked cardboard boxes. When I opened them, I discovered all forms of military ordnance inside. Included were dozens of rounds of high-caliber ammunition, various types of practice grenades, artillery shells, and several sticks of dynamite. Sitting in the wet basement, the munitions stockpile was unstable and a disaster waiting to happen.

After disarming the trip wire on the stairs, I recognized the ordnance as a concussion grenade. The explosion would not send out deadly shrapnel but rather a loud report that could cause burns and possible deafness in the enclosed environment. I made several trips to take the boxes outside and away from the house, but I was not sure what effect the sunlight might have in triggering a reaction, so I kept my distance once they were laid out on the lawn.

Disposing of the munitions was a job I was not ready to take on, so I considered turning the problem over to the sheriff's department. However, I was never comfortable with the local law enforcement because of the way they had handled previous investigations. I also knew the good-old-boy network did not care much for the outsiders who moved in from the big city. In addition, I learned that several officers were high school classmates of the father and probably would come to his defense if any criminal action were taken. Possession is nine-tenths of the law, and we owned the house. I felt more comfortable turning the ammunition over to the township police in my neighborhood, where I knew the chief and most of his deputies.

Looking back years later, I realized it was a dumb decision to move these unstable munitions 30 miles by car, when the slightest jolt could have created a catastrophe. My son also reminds me he was in charge of holding the boxes on his lap as we headed toward Columbus. Obviously we made it and the local police were notified. I think the patrolman they sent was expecting to pick up some discarded firecrackers or similar non-lethal explosives, but the expression on his face changed and he called for back-up once he peered into the boxes. After a flurry of activity, the bomb squad took away the munitions and the neighborhood settled back to normalcy. I told others only that I had found a cache of weapons in the cellar of an abandoned farmhouse I had purchased. I did not need an unstable person back in my life, and I was relieved when I found a buyer for my share of the farm a short time later.

As a follow-up, I kept one of the smaller explosive devices, and a neighbor and I tested its power by taping it to a small tree in his yard. With a wire attached to the pin, we ducked into his garage and gave a hard yank. After a flash and deafening roar we peered out from the garage and through the haze we saw the tree had all but disintegrated.

BUSINESS APPLICATION: FLEXIBILITY (CAN YOU ADJUST TO CHANGE IN A TIMELY FASHION?)

Bundled together, a common theme emerges from the events that took place on the previous pages: expect the unexpected and be ready to adjust. Never be so inflexible that you do not have a backup plan in place. This is especially true when operating a business. Everything is running smoothly when suddenly a key employee quits, you lose a valuable client, or an untimely audit from the IRS occurs. Sometimes you cannot predict the unforeseen, so you must prepare for it the best you can.

Several years ago, I was in the office of the president of a medium-size Midwestern bank, discussing an updated pension plan for his employees. The banker had spent several weeks at a computer school and was boasting in jest that with his newfound knowledge he would be able to uncover any employees who might have embezzled money from the bank. I had a good laugh over his comment, but the next day his longtime personal secretary, who had been in the room with us, turned herself in by admitting to stealing more than six figures from the financial institution. She had gotten in debt, so she "borrowed" some cash with the intent of paying it back. The debt snowballed and so did her borrowing, which went on for years. Chances were good she might never have been caught except for the comments made by her boss. She hoped confessing in advance of getting caught would help lighten her sentence.

Little of the stolen money was recovered, but the bank had an insurance policy that helped with the losses. The insurance was the bank's backup plan to cover the unexpected and keep the organization in good standing with the regulators. A successful business would be wise to consider adding insurance coverage as a Plan B to help ease the blow of unforeseen events.

Having the foresight to shift gears helped me land a large account when I was confronted with an almost impossible sales scenario. I was introducing a new employee benefit package to a financial institution. One hundred percent participation from the staff was necessary to make the program succeed. Management would be sharing in the cost of the program should it be implemented, but they felt confident that at least a few of the employees would not sign on, thus terminating the program and saving the bank the additional expenses.

I had to weigh two courses of action in my sales approach. The financial institution suggested I present the benefit plan to management first, so if one or more did not sign up, I would not have wasted much time in the process and the enrollment could be terminated. However, should they all participate, getting the rest of the staff committed would be easier. The alternative was to talk to each of the 100 employees first, a much more daunting task that would require total approval.

Since the bank had not endorsed the benefit plan, I decided to get the numbers on my side. The more difficult the task, the greater the reward was my focus in spending the next two weeks enrolling participants. Because they were contributing some of their own money, not everything went smoothly. A handful did not want to get involved, but knowing the program would collapse without their commitment, they succumbed to peer pressure. Others wanted to talk it over with their spouse, which is usually the kiss of death and a delaying tactic in any sales presentation. I would ask them if their better half had ever made a purchase without their approval, which often led to a quick signature. After the open enrollment period had ended, all of the employees had committed.

With this rousing endorsement of the program, I turned my attention to management, confident the final few sign-ups would be easy. It did not take long before the first bank officer I talked with revealed his negativity toward the enrollment. Cost for him and the bank were the main stumbling blocks in his reasoning not to commit. I had spent too much time and effort to be deterred by his objections and negativity. I showed him the participation results from the bank employees and how they were willing to use some of their hard-earned money to help fund this valuable benefit. If management did not enroll, it would sabotage the entire plan and have an effect on employee morale. Confronted with the possibility of a disgruntled staff, each officer decided to sign the agreement.

Without the leverage I had with the employees, the program would never have gotten off the ground. The more sensible approach of targeting management first would have resulted in failure, whereas using a more unorthodox sales mentality turned out to be the key. Sometimes a resilient attitude will guide you in the right direction.

TROPICAL MISHAPS

10

Trouble In Paradise

Vacations should be a time for fun, relaxation, and a chance to experience new wonders of the world without putting your life in jeopardy. A few years ago, I was hiking a section of the Bright Angel Trail at the Grand Canyon's southern rim when I heard rocks falling. I was fortunate to be near an outcropping of stones and ducked for cover as the boulders rumbled by. I was hoping the hikers below me could find adequate shelter in time to avoid a catastrophe. After the last rocks had passed, I decided not to press my luck and headed back up the trail to the rim. Reaching the top, I witnessed what had caused the mini-avalanche. Park rangers were escorting several men to a waiting van as a crowd of tourists gathered to watch. Apparently the men had decided to illegally rappel down the canyon wall, ignoring all warning signs, and dislodging rocks on their descent. They would face stiff fines, but the penalty could have been much worse if injuries or death had resulted from their stupidity.

On another occasion, while flying to Tucson, Arizona, with my family for spring break, I became increasingly ill with a fever, chills, and a bladder infection. Nothing is more unpleasant than continually running to the restroom during a five-hour flight. I thought the St. Patrick's Day celebration earlier in the week was finally catching up with me and I was now paying the price. After landing in Tucson, I checked in at an urgent care facility, received some antibiotics, and spent the rest of the week going through the motions of having fun.

Arriving back home, I learned several others in our party had come down with the same symptoms, and we discovered the green beer we had been drinking at a local watering hole had been altered. Apparently the Irish pub had run out of green food coloring and substituted green watercolor paint. Food poisoning and other infections resulted, and after numerous complaints, the health department shut down the pub. It goes without saying that green beer is no longer on my list of beverages when welcoming in the Irish holiday.

My brother and I jointly own a condo located in Crystal River, Florida, which is known as the manatee capital of the world. Each winter, as the Gulf of Mexico gets colder, thousands of these sea cows seek warmer waters by swimming up the river to the numerous springs that remain at a constant temperature. During this migration, boat navigation on the river is restricted to protect these gentle giants from the ravages of propeller blades, collisions, and other misfortunes orchestrated by humans.

To view the manatees up close, kayaks and canoes were recommended, so we rented a couple of kayaks and set our course to catch up with the annual pilgrimage. Because the boats sit only inches from the water line and the river is murky, it was hard to see these half-ton creatures until we were on top of them. Manatees, however, can stay submerged for only a few minutes before surfacing for air, so bubbles and penetrating nostrils help give away their locations.

We were paddling upriver when my brother spotted a large contingent of cows directly ahead. Without waiting for me to catch up, he guided his kayak toward the group and stopped in the center of the churning waters. Each mammal, including the babies, was marked with jagged scars across their backs, testifying to the many encounters they had with boat propellers. This is the reason why manatees do not like to be touched, especially from above.

So what did my brother do? He took his paddle and swept it over the back of a large manatee that was close to him. The cow broke the water's surface, triggering the rest to follow in a wild stampede of multi-ton mammals, and I was directly in their path. If one or more had landed on my kayak I most likely would have been crushed under their enormous weight. As fortune would have it, however, they dove under my craft just before reaching me. Still, the turbulence that was created almost threw me overboard and into the panicking mass.

Wet and shaken, I had a few choice words for my brother, who was already searching for another pod to stir up. He commented if I were crushed to death, the local chamber of commerce would pay him big money to keep the incident quiet. After all, manatees were the town's main tourist attraction, and if word got out that people could be killed by these gentle beasts, it could spell financial disaster for the industry.

A few years ago, my late wife Amy and I flew to Hawaii to visit her aunt who lived on a sugarcane plantation located on the side of an extinct volcano. Before heading to Maui, where the aunt and her husband resided, we decided to spend a few days on Kauai and explore the small island. Except for a chain of mountains on the north coast, we could drive almost around the entire island from either direction in a couple of days, so we planned our stay at a resort near the midway point.

The hotel was on a small bay and although it had a salt-water pool, we had come to Hawaii to swim in the warm, emerald-green ocean that bordered the resort. The small, rocky beach did not measure up to the pictures in the brochure, and we should have taken noticed there was an absence of swimmers cavorting in the surf as we made a mad dash into the tepid waters. Almost immediately I felt a sharp pain in the heel of my right foot as I realized that the ocean floor was a conglomerate of jagged volcanic rock and coral. There were no signs posted that this section of the beach was off-limit to swimmers. As I exited the surf, I saw the water where I had been standing was turning a pastel, pinkish color from the blood I was losing. The rocks had opened a large gash on my heel and I limped toward a lifeguard stationed by the hotel's pool. The cut was deep and would have required stitches if located anywhere other than the heel. The best the guard could do was to spray the wound with an antiseptic and wrap it tightly. He cautioned that because of the warm tropical waters, strep bacteria in the wound could pose the greatest danger. To minimize infection, the heel had to be cleansed several times daily and the ocean was off-limits. This minor setback was not going to ruin the trip, so with a handful of pain pills and a bloody tennis shoe, I limped my way around the islands playing tourist with Amy.

  The next day, Amy and I headed north to explore the Na Pali Coast. On the drive back to the hotel, we passed a stretch of sand on the ocean where the movie *South Pacific* had been filmed some 30 years previously. The beach was deserted except for a few young Hawaiian boys who were playing on a makeshift raft at the month of a small river. We wore bathing suits under our clothes and decided it would be fun to recreate history by swimming in the same surf where the movie was filmed. I forgot about the advice that the lifeguard gave me as I stepped into the ocean, which dropped off suddenly from the beach into chest-high water.

  Unlike most Hawaiian beaches, where we could wade out for several yards before we reached deep waters, this encounter with the ocean came as a surprise. Because we were both excellent swimmers, there was no cause for alarm, even though we could feel a strong undertow. After a few minutes, we decided to exit the water only to find we could not gain a foothold in the steep bank and soft sands. Each wave created a riptide that pulled us away from shore and farther out to sea. After several futile attempts, the reality set in that where we had entered the ocean was not going to be our exit.

Less experienced swimmers would have fought the current until exhaustion, thus putting their lives in jeopardy, but Amy and I tread water as we surveyed the coastline for a means of escape. The boys on the raft were about 100 yards down the beach, so we decided to swim in their direction. As we approached, I noticed that the river flowing into the surf had some bushes we could grab onto. The river was much colder than the ocean, and the current was swift as we struggled to reach the mouth and pull ourselves up the muddy embankment, much to the amusement of the native boys who were watching our drama unfold.

Cold and exhausted, we collected our clothes and headed for the car when I happened to notice a number of handmade white crosses decorating a section of the beach. Upon closer inspection, we realized the markers were in memory of the people who had drowned in the waters where we had been swimming. We had also missed a large sign warning bathers about dangerous riptides and undertows. *South Pacific* may have been filmed at this location, but the swimming scenes most likely were shot elsewhere.

The rest of our Hawaiian vacation was not quite as adventuresome, except for our visit with Amy's Aunt Helen and a trip through the sugarcane fields. Helen and her husband Neil lived in a small home halfway up the side of an extinct volcano on the island of Maui. Neil was a retired minister and writer who used Maui as a base to pursue several interesting hobbies. Reportedly he is one of a handful of people who have hiked around the entire coastline of the five major Hawaiian Islands, except where the mountains make it impassable. In addition, he has played the signature hole on the top 50 most famous golf courses of his era. As the story goes, the only course that prohibited Neil from reaching his goal was Augusta National, home of the Masters Tournament; that is, until the great Bobby Jones himself, a founding member of the Club, interceded and allowed Neil to complete his mission.

The couple's house was surrounded by cane fields and quite isolated, so Helen kept a large dog for protection when her husband was away. The canine was believed to be part wolf and, upon our arrival, greeted us with teeth bared and hair bristling on its back. We stayed frozen in the car until Helen, who was barely five feet tall, arrived and placed a chain on the collar of the dog, whom she had affectingly named "Chemo."

Once Chemo was secure, we made a hasty retreat to the safety of the house, or so we thought. Each night after we went to bed, Chemo was let in and would head directly to our room. A locked door did not deter his aggressiveness and the demonic animal would spend the better part of each night clawing and chewing on the door's outer frame. For fear he would somehow get in, Amy and I moved a large piece of bedroom furniture in front of the door each night and equipped the room with several makeshift urinals since a midnight trip to the bathroom was out of the question. We would venture out from our barricaded cell only after Chemo was put outside in the morning. Our car was parked between Chemo and the house, so each morning we had to run the gantlet with the beast in hot pursuit. Even though we had free room and board and enjoyed Helen's company, we cut our visit short for obvious reasons, including the lack of a good night's sleep.

One last adventure on Maui occurred when I decided to take a shortcut through a large sugarcane field. The island is bisected by the main highway that travels between the two coastlines, with road connections at each end. We could see Aunt Helen's farm from the road below, but we had to drive a dozen miles out of our way before we could double back and connect to the road that went up the volcano. Sugarcane crops dotted the landscape between the highway and the mountain road, but occasionally there was a dirt trail that would disappear into the fields. Although the trails were posted with "No Trespassing" signs, I decided to chance it and headed the car down one of the dirt roads toward Aunt Helen's farm in the distance. Amy was apprehensive about my decision but stayed quiet as the tall cane stalks closed in on all sides. It was a Sunday afternoon, so I figured we would encounter few, if any, workers in the fields.

After traveling for about five minutes, I noticed that a helicopter was circling above us and shouting something over a loudspeaker. As I was lowering the window, several military vehicles suddenly appeared out of the cane fields and blocked the road. Men in olive fatigues jumped out of the jeeps with an arsenal of weapons pointed at our car. Apparently the dust from our vehicle gave us away as the helicopter pinpointed our location and radioed it to the cars below. Amy was sure the end was near as the car came to a screeching halt and we were ordered to exit the vehicle. The officer in charge instructed us to put our hands on the hood while other uniformed men searched our car. The front and back seats were torn out, the spare tire in the trunk was ejected, and mirrors on poles were used to search the car's underbelly. Finding nothing of interest, the officer got on the radio and shortly thereafter the helicopter and some of the soldiers left.

It was explained to us that drug dealers were using the cane fields to hide their marijuana plants and therefore the fields were under 24-hour surveillance. Anyone in the area was there illegally and subject to arrest. I envisioned spending the rest of our vacation behind bars, paying a hefty fine, or both. Amy was emotionally shaken and appeared to be going into shock. She has never even had a parking ticket and now the prospect of being a felon started to sink in. The officer in charge took notice of her distress and decided to let us off the hook with a stern warning. Back in the car, I asked if we could continue down the road since we were almost to our destination. I was told in no uncertain terms "to turn the car around and head back to where you entered the fields." The police got no further arguments from me. That night at a local tavern, Amy, who was a nondrinker, found comfort in a couple of gin and tonics.

BUSINESS APPLICATION: DECISIVENESS (ARE YOU RESOLUTE IN YOUR DECISION MAKING)?

Several times during our Hawaii trip I was presented with a situation where a decision had to be made quickly, without hesitation. Fighting riptides and dodging a partially washed out narrow road climbing toward an extinct volcano on Maui called for decisive action, or otherwise certain peril was imminent.

Back in the 1980s, investment advisers compiled a list of the 50 most popular stocks that should be included in every client's portfolio. Called the "Nifty Fifty," these blue-chip winners, with such names as Pan Am, Westinghouse, and Merrill Lynch, were household brands that were considered safe. Today, less than half of these securities are still in existence, with many losing a substantial portion of their original value. Mergers, acquisitions, and in many cases, bankruptcy were the reasons these companies disappeared from the original list.

The current list includes many of the high-flying tech companies, energy, and financial institutions, and if history repeats itself, most will not be around 30 years from now. Accelerated changes are making products obsolete overnight.

Every investment house will tell you to invest for the long term, but that does not mean purchasing a stock and then forgetting about it. They also will tell you what to look for when buying securities, but few advise you about when to sell. It goes against human nature to admit that you made a poor decision, and even harder to pull the trigger and sell at a loss.

Don't fall in love with a company and ignore the warning signs. Ask yourself if you would buy this same company today, compared to the time you originally made the purchase. If the answer is "no," then be decisive and sell immediately, rather than end up like the many investors that waited too long with their Nifty Fifty portfolios.

I have established several guidelines when considering an investment opportunity. First, I avoid very low price securities or "penny stocks." They are low for a reason, and they can be easily manipulated. I also avoid boiler room salesmen who are pitching a particular stock over the phone. I figure if the stock had any real promise, the shares would have been snapped up by savvy investors long before my name came up on their call sheets. Last, I stay away from companies that hype their name in print or on their website promising a can't-miss opportunity with such catch phrases as "breakthrough," "huge potential," or "you must act quickly."

These over-the-top promotions are solely for the benefit of the company and are targeting the unsophisticated investor who is more interested in a get-rich-quick deal than taking time to do the homework that improves their financial position.

I have nothing against most financial planners and investment advisers, but many target their services to clients after the clients have already become successful. Where were they when you had little money to invest but needed their guidance? If an adviser's fee schedule is based on a percentage of your minuscule portfolio, chances are he will look for more lucrative opportunities rather than help you grow your investments.

Once you have achieved financial success, I find it ironic that an adviser will call and offer his services to help manage your money. Unless you lack the interest or are too busy with other endeavors to watch over your investments, why pay someone a fee now, when they were not around to help when you were building your estate?

11
South Of the Border

Being an owner, partner, or investor in numerous business ventures over the course of my life, I must say not all were a success. The companies I had a controlling interest in did much better than those with others at the helm making the critical decisions. As an entrepreneur, I expected all of my business endeavors to be successful since I don't invest time and money in a company with the expectation of failure.

Sometimes, however, doing everything right is not enough. Even with a solid business plan, a strong revenue stream, and a revolutionary concept, expanding too rapidly into unfamiliar territory where unforeseen events take place can lead to the company's demise. Such a failure occurred at a grand opening ceremony for a corporate event in a Caribbean country when the local government decided to step in. Families, including mine, who were there to participate, had to make a hasty retreat and return to the States.

During the Seventies, I was one of several regional directors to help promote the concept of a national putting championship in which all amateur golfers could enter for the chance of winning a sizable cash award. Putting is the great equalizer in the game of golf, so women as well as men could compete for the grand prize. The company made money by charging an entry fee for golfers to participate in one of the organized tournaments held at country clubs around the nation. Winners of those tournaments—and their families—were invited to compete in the finals at a luxurious resort.

At the resort, special putting greens, consisting of 18 holes, were laid out in conjunction with the club's own golf course. Each green was designed to be a replica of one of the world's best-known venues, such as Pebble Beach and Augusta, with similar pin placements, undulations, and adjoining sand traps. The tournament would run the better part of a week, and the last two days would be covered by a national television sports network. Meanwhile, the family members could enjoy the many amenities the resort had to offer.

The inaugural tournament was scheduled to be held on Grand Bahama Island, but a last-minute glitch required us to shift the event to another Caribbean island. A well-known professional golfer welcomed us to his country club, where the tournament would be held.

My family and I flew onto the island a few days before the festivities were to begin and stayed at a beautiful hillside villa overlooking the course and the Caribbean. The accommodations included a maid, cook, and pool attendant; all of them helped to define the word "luxury." My wife Lynne and the kids spent most of the day around the pool, while I prepared for the upcoming tournament.

On the second evening at the villa, I noticed someone walking around the pool, so I went outside to investigate. I was confronted by a rather short, stocky man dressed in military fatigues and carrying an assault rifle. Repeated questions went unanswered, and I concluded he could not understand English.

What stood out in our encounter was that his smile was laced with two rows of shiny gold teeth.

Getting nowhere in the conversation, I called the main clubhouse and was informed that our paramilitary intruder had been sent there for our protection against roving gangs that came up from the city to loot the villas and rob foreign tourists. He was a native from an area in the interior of the island and was a descendant of criminals who were exiled there. In the morning, he faded back into the hills, but he reappeared each evening in total silence.

My wife was not comfortable with the armed stranger around our children, but I felt his presence was better than the alternative, so we adjusted to the situation. I became more suspicious about our bodyguard, however, when I noticed that the other villas in the area, although vacant, did not have guards at night to protect against break-ins.

The next day, a man appeared at our villa offering donkey rides for the children, in return for a small fee. He was also armed, and I was beginning to think this must be the norm for the island. We let the kids have their ride but made sure they did not leave the villa grounds.

The day before the start of the tournament, Lynne and I were enjoying lunch while the children played outside. Suddenly we heard a loud explosion coming from the pool area. Rushing out to find the kids, we met the pool attendant, who informed us he was mixing a combination of chloride and other chemicals for treating the water, and vapors from the concoction had detonated. No one was hurt, but the incident made us far less comfortable in our surroundings.

That evening our family was invited to dinner at the home of the island's minister of tourism. The home was located on the outskirts of the city and was surrounded by a high wall and an iron gate; the enclosed courtyard was covered with lush tropical vegetation, and the estate had all the amenities, including a pool. Our host had children similar in age to ours, so while they were busy playing outside, the minister and I went over the final details for the next day's big event.

Just before dinner, there was a commotion outside, and the children rushed into the house. Each one was excitedly telling a different version of what had transpired, so the minister and I went out to investigate. Lying in the courtyard was a bloody headless chicken someone had thrown over the wall. I surmised it must have been some harmless prank; however, the look on the minister's face revealed that the act was a more serious matter. Once we were inside, he explained that the symbolism associated with a decapitated chicken dated back to the days of voodoo and was a warning sign about impending trouble. We ate a hurried dinner, said our goodbyes, and were escorted back to our villa, where our nightly armed guard was nowhere to be seen.

An early-morning phone call from the villa's rental office informed us to pack quickly and wait for a car that would take us to the airport. The representative emphasized the resort couldn't guarantee our safety should we decide to stay. I asked about the tournament, which was scheduled to start that day, and I was told the event had been canceled. No explanation was ever given, but due to the political unrest in the country, which was run by a leftist-leaning government, uprisings and revolutions were fairly common. All the equipment, monies, and materials needed to put on the tournament were confiscated by the local authorities, officially putting us out of business.

The insurrection, rebellion, or whatever it was called, lasted only a few days, but the damage had already been done. The losses not only extended to the company but to the participants as well. They had a financial interest in the tournament, which was lost, and even if somehow the business survived, it would have been difficult to convince the public to get involved again.

Adding a safety net, including business interruption, liability, and foreign travel insurance, might not have saved the company, but it would have helped lessen the financial burden and allowed us all to sleep better at night.

On our flight back to the States we encountered one last obstacle as we approached Hartsfield International Airport in Atlanta. A tornado had touched down near one of the runways, and our aircraft was diverted to a holding pattern over western Georgia. For the next hour, we rode out one of the most violent thunderstorms and winds that I have ever witnessed, including during military service. The kids got sick, my wife was freaking out, and I was positive lightning had struck the plane at least once. When we were finally cleared to land, a roar of relief came from the passengers. As we disembarked through Customs, an agent tried to segregate our children, confusing air sickness with some strange disease they might be bringing in from a foreign country. After many of the passengers showed similar symptoms, the agent and pilot concurred about the illness being the result of the turbulent flight, and we were allowed to proceed through the terminal. The United States and home never looked better.

As a footnote, our gracious host, the minister of tourism and his family, immigrated to the United States shortly after the insurrection and ended up running a lucrative travel agency in Florida.

Upon further reflection, I realized the directors had taken their eyes off the main objective of running a putting tournament, and instead had ventured off course into the travel industry. If our contest had been held at a resort in the United States rather than a developing country, chances are the national putting championships would still be going strong today.

FOCUS (CAN YOU KEEP YOUR EYE ON THE BALL?)

The story illustrates how risk can be significantly magnified if your business strays from the familiar and into uncharted territories. No amount of expertise or planning can save a company if it wanders too far out of its comfort zone. Some of the most promising business ventures can go belly up by not following a proven road map. Familiarity with trusted products, name recognition, and brands can help minimize risk and channel success in different directions. This concept was illustrated in a stock-picking contest, held for grade school students several years ago.

When my late wife Amy was teaching fifth grade at a suburban school in Columbus, she invited me to her classroom to teach the students about investing in the market. I set up a weekly course that would run for six months and, to make it interesting, we made a contest part of the lesson plan. We divided the class into equal groups, with each student group receiving $10,000 in fictitious money. They were to research a portfolio of stocks they could purchase with their money, based on the current prices listed in the New York Stock Exchange or other venues. There was no limit as to the number of shares or types of stocks purchased as long as the groups did not go over their cash allotment. At the end of the six-month period, the team whose portfolio had the largest increase in value would be the winner and receive a prize.

Interest in the contest was such that several team members begged their parents to subscribe to the *Wall Street Journal* so they could follow the progress of their stocks. These requests did not sit well with the families since they knew very little about investing and had better uses for their money. Each group's stock picks were kept secret, but weekly updates informed the class on how the contest was going. As in real life, some buyers stayed the course, while others bought and sold stock regularly, trying to time the actions in the market.

At the end of the six-month contest, the winning team's portfolio had more than doubled in value. The students in the group did not have a secret formula for picking the winners. They instead picked stocks of companies that they were familiar with and enjoyed visiting. Brand names such as McDonald's,

STRADDLING THE ABYSS

Gap, and Disney beat out more exotic equities that were featured in trade journals or as the hot tip of the week. One of the students on the winning team suggested that instead of the prize, he would settle for the profits that the portfolio generated. I informed him since he had no skin in the game as far as real money was concerned, he could choose between fake dollars or the prize. He elected to take the prize.

Winners and losers alike were enthusiastic about the mechanics behind the markets and how they could make money by investing well. However, the lack of support from many of the families and the negativity they attached to this form of "gambling" doomed the project for other classes. The families could not focus on how investing affected their everyday lives, whether it be retirement, interest rates, inflation cost, or other factors. Sometimes ignorance is *not* bliss when education is at stake.

The Rain Forest Below

During the summer of 2016, part of my family traveled to a five-star resort located on the shores of the Pacific Ocean in Costa Rica. For seven days, we sampled the local cuisine, hiked the beaches, and partook of some of the numerous activities available to resort guests. One such adventure involved a zip-lining tour through the nearby rain forest, where we anticipated the wildlife would be plentiful. My family signed up for the tour at the hotel, but I decided to wait until we were actually on location to survey the course before making a commitment.

The next morning, a small van met our party in front of the hotel and transported us a few miles up a steep, narrow road to a lodge that sat several hundred feet above sea level. The view was spectacular, and the inside of the lodge had all the modern comforts, including a dining area, bar, and gift shop. There was very little vegetation around the barren facilities, as most of the jungle canopy stretched out below us. I should have picked up on the fact that the zip lines were not going through the forest but above them. Four sets of steel cables extended from a small wooden platform on a hill across a valley to another platform about one-quarter mile away. Thus we would be zip-lining in pairs along the various routes. Since the course did not appear to be that intimidating, I decided to join the rest of my family for the tour rather than spend the next several hours in the bar, which had yet to open.

A team of Spanish-speaking instructors using broken English ushered us outside, where we joined a small group of other riders who were already suited up. We each received a hard hat, heavy leather gloves, and a harness we stepped into and securely tightened. After a short lesson on safety and how to operate the zip line, we were good to go. I, along with my son Johnny, who barely made the weight limit, were picked to make the first descent. When he asked the instructors how much weight the cables could hold, they replied that a small elephant could probably make it. Needless to say, Johnny was not pleased with the comparison.

We were literally pushed off the platform, and with an adrenaline rush I settled back in the harness with my hands tightly gripping the steering bar for the short but exhilarating ride. As I approached the lower platform, my speed had not lessened. I was coming in too hot. Suddenly a sharp jolt threw me up and backward as the pulley hit the tension spring on the cable. The shock threw off my approach, and I did not get my legs up high enough before crashing into the platform. Both kneecaps hit the wooden structure; I was sure they were shattered as the team operator pulled me aboard. After being helped to my feet, I was unhooked from the cable and relieved that the pain in my legs had subsided.

Johnny was not quite as fortunate, as his instructor backed away just before impact, and Johnny went crashing into the platform wall. Costa Rica men are generally slightly built, and they are not eager to put themselves in harm's way when a large human projectile is barreling toward them. As my son described it, the catcher responded like a matador, gracefully stepping aside as the bull went charging past. Outside of a few scrapes and bruises, we both survived the initial impact and stood by as the rest of the party made their descent without further incident.

As we all congratulated each other on our accomplishments, the instructors informed us this zip run was just a warm-up for what lay ahead. Our group was transported in an all-terrain vehicle farther up the mountain to a windswept vista nearly 1,000 feet above sea level. Stretched out below were the rain forest, Pacific, and our resort, which was just a small cluster of buildings in the distance. Three of the instructors hooked up to the pulleys and descended from the mountain, disappearing into a canopy of trees nearly a mile away. Meanwhile, the other guides were instructing our group on the Superman technique of zip-lining.

Rather than sitting down and holding onto the pulley handle, we were placed on our stomachs with the harness attached to our backs. To create stability, our legs were securely tied together and a heavy weighted vest was placed over our shoulders. With limited movement, I felt like a hogtied animal heading toward my demise. We would be descending more than 500 feet at speeds nearing 70 miles per hour, so line sway had to be kept at a minimum. Again in barely understandable English, the instructor told us to keep our arms outstretched with thumbs pointed up during the first part of the fall but to bring our arms in tight to our bodies when we neared the platform. Otherwise the post supporting the narrow landing area could easily snap off an exposed upper limb.

Swinging beneath the cable, I tried to avoid looking over the platform so vertigo would not set in as the guides prepared for launch. Instead of a push, the guides catapulted me over the edge in a slingshot motion that sent me into a brief free fall before I felt the harness tighten around my body. The jungle below was just a blur as I accelerated towards an unknown target hidden somewhere in the woods ahead. The combination of speed and weight made it impossible to raise my head, so I had no idea how close I was to the platform. Disaster was averted when I suddenly heard frantic cries in Spanish and on cue put my arms to my sides. A split second later I hit the tension spring and fell onto the platform.

The descent took less than 30 seconds, and with the focus on the landing area, coupled with the speed, I did not have a chance to think about the what-ifs. Still, I was sweating profusely and exhausted from the weights I was carrying. The vest and leg ropes were removed and I climbed to the next platform. There was no time to relax or wait for the rest of the group to catch up since the launch area accommodated only two riders and the steep drop-offs around the platforms could put the other people in jeopardy. Thus, as my Costa Rica guide stated, "The assembly line must keep moving."

The phase-three run on the zip line reverted to the traditional harness and seat arrangement, which made it easier for me to steer and see where I was headed. The distance was equal to the Superman run, but with the reduced speed I could sit back and finally enjoy the tropical wonderland below. I was thinking that the worst part of the trip was behind me when a strong gust of wind came through the mountain pass and twisted my harness and pulley sideways, leaving me stranded about 50 meters from the platform. I was dangling and swaying in the wind above the valley floor, not able to move in any direction. One of the instructors called out from the platform with a sense of urgency in his voice telling me not to move, which I found ironic since I couldn't go anywhere.

Strangely, I felt a serene calm as I surveyed the landscape below, not realizing I was in more peril than I thought. The harness was twisted in an odd shape and the pulley was partially detached from the cable. The instructors on the platform shouted encouragement as they planned a rescue attempt. My concern was that another zip-liner might be rushing toward me and the collision would knock us both off of the cable. My daughter informed me later that the guides had two-way radios and they were told a rescue was in progress and to shut down the lines.

One of the smaller members of the zip-line crew, with rope in hand, monkey-climbed from the platform along the cable until he was positioned above me. I tied the rope around my waist while the other end was secured to a post near the landing area. I guessed the 50-meter drop before the rope took hold would be my security blanket. We had to pull in unison along the cable line back toward the platform. The combination of wind and the dislodged pulley made the journey painfully slow; we were moving only about six inches on each attempt. After 10 minutes of strenuous exercise, we finally reached the platform. I was exhausted and my arms felt like dead weights, but there was no time for rest as the delay had created a logjam of zip-liners behind me.

I was thankful that the fourth and last descent was non-eventful, but one more surprise awaited me at the final platform. After landing, I noticed the tower's height was still a number of yards from the ground with no exit route. I saw that the only way down was to bungee jump. A cord was attached to my harness and I was led to a small platform jutting out from the tower. A slight motivational push from the guide sent me free falling into space for a few seconds before the slack in the cord tightened, and I landed on a small mat that helped cushion the drop. The ordeal was finally over and I was relieved to shed the harness and return to solid ground.

After everyone completed the course, we took the bus ride back up the mountain to the lodge for refreshments and the swapping of stories about our adventures. One of the instructors was the photographer for the group, and the pictures had already been developed for purchase. My packet included numerous shots of the descent but none of the rescue from the cable. When I questioned the photographer about the missing pictures, he stated that those types of photos adversely affected their business model. Later I learned from a brochure that this particular zip-line course was one of the fastest, longest, and most challenging of all similar operations in Central and South America. If I had read this information beforehand, I probably would have ended up with an expensive bar tab.

BUSINESS APPLICATION: PREPAREDNESS (ARE YOU READY FOR EVERY POSSIBILITY?)

The message resonating from this experience, which sadly I did not follow, was preparedness. I had my own vision of riding a zip-line through the jungle canopy at a leisurely pace, photographing all types of colorful birds and mammals along the way. In reality, if I had studied the brochure and asked questions of the guides, I could have turned the unexpected into a more enjoyable experience. Likewise, with all successful business models, preparedness is the key when confronting the challenges of the unknown head on.

Being organized to a state of readiness also applies when purchasing or investing in a company. The typical due diligence approach is to evaluate the business's value and prospects for the future. The numbers are crunched; balance sheets, profit and loss statements along with other financial data are held under a microscope; and the products and management team are scrutinized. This activity is usually the drill when determining a fair purchase price for the buyout. When necessary, I also like to look under the hood in search of red flags.

Starting with management, I search for the reasons why they need an influx of cash as an investment or for the purchase of their company. Will the money be used to expand and grow the business, or is it earmarked to help pay off large debts that have accumulated through loans from creditors? Bailing out a company laden in debt is one of the red flags to look for.

Is management or the owner putting themselves ahead of the company, by channeling any profits toward their own salaries, benefits, and stock options at the expense of the business and their employees? Has the CEO enriched himself with a "golden parachute" should there be a buyout or if he is let go after a merger?

Does management have enough equity in the game so they would have the most to lose should their business fail?

Other red flags center on the products or services a company is trying to market. Many new businesses start out with an idea, but little capital or a marketing plan to make it successful. Money alone will not save a company if the other business blocks are not in place. Most start-up companies want to succeed, but a few are interested only in getting their investments back no matter who foots the bill. This can happen if the company has one product generating the bulk of their sales and it starts to run out of steam. If the business does not have a wide enough moat so competitors would have difficulty encroaching on the concept, or if the product is not protected by patents and there are no other innovative products or services in the pipeline, then look for a bailout from the management team.

To help minimize the risk associated with any investment, it is important to be familiar with the products and services the company is offering. For example, if you are not tech savvy, investing large sums in an IT company may not be your smartest move. However, if a business I am interested in can control its debt, have excellent cash flow, boast an intriguing product line, and demonstrate it can have consistent earning power through a strong management team, then I may make an investment decision in one of three ways.

Preferably, I will become a silent partner and let management remain in control of the day-to-day operations. It is a win-win for both groups, as I will not be tied down and will have time to pursue other interests, and the employees can continue along the path that has made their business successful without the fear of being micromanaged or let go.

Occasionally, I will position myself in the role of a limited partner, and therefore "limit" my exposure to potential loses or liabilities. I will have priority in receiving any profits or tax deductions and share in the success of the enterprise. My voting powers, however, will be restricted, especially when it comes to removing a general partner. It is extremely important to have full disclosure about the partnership in the prospectus.

Least favorable, from my point of view, is taking over the operations of a business through the purchase of majority shares or buying out the owner. My time will be completely absorbed in the daily operations and my hands tied should a better investment opportunity present itself. My objective is to grow the business as quickly as possible and make it attractive for a venture capitalist, outside firm, or even the employees to purchase my holdings, hopefully at a profit if I have properly prepared myself.

MY REAL-LIFE ADVENTURES ARE TAME IN COMPARISON TO THE NEXT STORY

13
Life In the Balance

As much as I have learned from the perils that have placed my life and businesses at risk, these lessons pale when compared to the everyday struggles that Amy, my friend, partner, and wife had to endure to survive each day. Imagine putting your trust in the hands of others so you can breathe, eat, and function with a body that is almost totally immobile. But Amy, for more than twelve years, met these challenges with grace, determination, and an unwavering positive attitude. Friends and strangers said she was an inspiration to everyone she met; however, her reply was, "To heck with inspiration. I just want to get well."

Amy was a single mother raising two small girls; she possessed a gift for teaching and a zest for life. She loved the outdoors, especially around water, where she excelled at swimming and operating her sailboat. She was independent, adventurous, and competitive. Over the years, however, a neurological disorder slowly robbed her of her ability to walk, talk, and breathe on her own. She became dependent on a respirator and the nurses who were in charge of its operation.

Amy and I met on a blind date arranged by mutual friends, and although we did not have a lot in common, somehow we hit it off. She came from a large, close-knit family, where reunions were the norm each summer at her parents' cottage in Minnesota. Teaching was her passion; she worked both in the Columbus City Schools and at the Ohio School for the Deaf. In addition, she taught Sunday school, coached a deaf basketball team, and tutored learning-disabled children. Much of her free time was devoted to charitable causes.

Subtle hints that something was wrong with her body appeared after we had been dating for a couple of years. At a dance, she had trouble performing several routine moves with her feet, and later that year she had difficulty keeping up with the girls and me during a trip to the Magic Kingdom. A number of doctor-prescribed treatments brought no relief, so we decided on our next trip to Minnesota we would visit the Mayo Clinic in Rochester.

The clinic set up a week of testing, with each day's results used to eliminate the disorders she did *not* have. On the last day, the doctors came in with their findings. They seemed to be pleased with the results, so Amy and I assumed a simple solution to her problems was at hand. Neither of us comprehended the term "ALS" when the physicians used it to describe her illness. Only when they said "Lou Gehrig's Disease" did I realize the severity of the diagnosis. After being given a timetable of three and five years and no cure or treatments available, we returned to her cabin on Lake Minnetonka in a state of shock.

Once the reality sank in, I decided to research the disease we were fighting. The Mayo Clinic came up with the diagnosis, but I was looking for a hospital that specialized in neuromuscular disorders. The nearest clinic to my home was at the University of Chicago, so over the Thanksgiving weekend we made the trip to the Windy City. The doctors had read the

Mayo findings before our visit, and after a few short questions they said Amy had Spinal Muscular Atrophy, or SMA, rather than ALS. This disease primarily affects children, and although the symptoms are similar to ALS, the lifespan is much longer. Amy and I both assumed that with the extended time frame, research would come up with a cure or at least be able to slow down the progression of the disease. As I soon learned, however, this disease fell under the MDA umbrella and competed for limited dollars with dozens of other disorders. Amy faced a long journey of declining health with little hope a miracle cure would be found.

SMA has a cruel way of attacking and taking over the body. Amy was still able to function even with weakness in her feet, which slowed her down but did not impede her mobility. Then she would have muscle spasms in another part of her body and weakness would soon follow. Each time these spasms occurred, Amy would be consumed with depression, knowing that nerves were dying and she was creeping ever closer toward total immobility.

Even with the grim prognosis, Amy decided to make the most out of her situation. She continued teaching, and when her legs lost their mobility she ran her fifth-grade class from a wheelchair. This dedication earned her "Teacher of the Year" in the Columbus City Schools. When her arms gave out and she could no longer write, she used a voice-activated computer to communicate. And when the disease robbed Amy of her speech, she used the only muscles left in her body, her eyebrows, to painstakingly spell words on the computer. She even used this form of communication to write a series of children books about birds that frequented the many feeders in her back yard. In 1996, Amy was recognized as a "Community Hero" and together we carried the Olympic Torch on its way to Atlanta, Georgia.

As the disease progressed, Amy no longer had control of her life. Her independence was gone, replaced by a team of nurses, family members, and on occasion the local EMS, which would perform two vital functions: keeping her air passages and lungs cleared by suctioning out her trachea and making sure the respirator was operating properly. This was a 24/7 responsibility, but on occasion a crisis would arise.

Most weekends I would stay overnight at Amy's home, not only to keep her company, but also to be a backup when her regular nurses were off and new aides would fill in the shifts. Many were not familiar with Amy's needs, so I would conduct a crash course on procedures before turning the duties over to them. I slept in a bedroom upstairs but never fully rested, knowing a new nurse was on board and that Amy had similar anxieties.

On more than one occasion, I was awakened by a piercing sound that indicated Amy was not getting air through the respirator. The alarm went off if the power shut down and the backup failed, there was another malfunction, or if the breathing tube became detached from the trachea. From the moment the alarm sounded, we had less than a minute to fix the problem before Amy ran out of air. On one occasion, as I rushed downstairs, I passed the nurse, who was asleep on the couch. I hurried to the respirator and found the breathing tube had indeed separated; although Amy could not speak, the terrified look in her eyes revealed how fragile her life was and how dependent she was on others. I reattached the tube, and Amy's breathing came back on track. The noise of the alarm had had no effect whatsoever on the nurse, who was still in deep slumber and unaware of the tragedy that had almost unfolded and could have cost Amy her life.

Another factor that always had Amy and the nurses on edge was the weather. Amy's house was located in a subdivision with numerous old trees and exposed electrical lines. Even small storms would wreak havoc in the neighborhood, with fallen limbs and downed power lines being a constant possibility. Loss of electricity would shut down the respirator and the backup battery would kick in. If the power outage lasted a short time, there would be no problem, but in most cases the duration was several days.

To help reduce our anxiety, I purchased a gas generator as a backup. The problem was that the nurses could not leave Amy and go to the garage to start up the generator, so those duties fell on my shoulders. Since I lived about twenty minutes away, timing was critical. In numerous cases, the nurses waited too long, and the battery went dead before I received the call. The only choice left was to manually "bag" Amy by slowly pumping air into her lungs until help arrived. This process took precision, and not all the nurses mastered the procedure. A certain rhythm had to be maintained in bagging to coincide with her normal breathing patterns. If the pumping action was too fast or slow her lungs would collapse and suffocation could quickly follow.

Prolonged outages were especially stressful since the generator would eventually run out of gas even with a backup supply. If the power outage was widespread, it would make the pumps at nearby service stations useless, and I would have to scour the city for a source of fuel. The local fire department always helped by setting up their own generators for Amy should all else fail, and on rare occasions the EMS would transfer her to a nearby hospital so she could get the treatment she needed.

It is hard to imagine the stress Amy endured when storms rolled in or the alarm on her respirator sounded. Yet this became a part of her daily life for a number of years prior to her passing in 2005, shortly after we were married. She never surrendered herself to the affliction and her determination to fight against overwhelming odds serves as a testament for how each one of us should conduct our lives. Taped to the ceiling above her hospital bed was a sheet of paper that became known as "Amy's Creed." It was the first thing she saw when she awoke each morning and focused on when retiring in the evening. This one small piece of paper set the standards for how she conducted her life:

"Meditate, smile, laugh, and sing, being grateful for every moment of life."

"Work hard but play fair. Love others totally and forgive quickly."

"Find a bright spot on the horizon and keep it in focus until you reach it."

"Enjoy the simple beauty of nature that surrounds your everyday life."

"Bet on God because he is betting on you."

"Leave the world a better place because of your presence."

"The difficult I can do immediately; the impossible takes a little longer.

"Always have hope, and above all, never ever, ever give up."

LIFE APPLICATION: PERSEVERANCE (CAN YOU KEEP GOING, EVEN IN TOUGH CIRCUMSTANCES?)

Amy's resolve in the face of adversity is a lesson about living life to the fullest. For Amy, success was not measured in accumulated wealth or titles, but by the obstacles she had to overcome in trying to succeed. If you do your best, then that's success, and that makes Amy the most successful person I have ever known.

Epilogue

It is not uncommon for other people to stereotype a successful person as "lucky." They also use luck to rationalize why they aren't getting the big breaks or missed out on a promotion. A recent study conducted by a major university sought to ascertain why some people seem to have a lucky streak while others are less fortunate. The study result was that certain people prepare to be lucky. The saying "the harder I work the luckier I get" is just part of the equation, but this group also creates possibilities, is open to new ideas, follow hunches, and assumes manageable risk. They view every setback as an opportunity and possess an optimistic attitude in the face of adversity. They define financial independence not as making more money, but in using their abilities and positions to enhance the lives and success of others. As far as their children are concerned, they generally agree with Warren Buffet's philosophy: You should leave your children enough so they can do anything with their lives, but not enough so they can do nothing.

When he was the manager of a variety store in Detroit, my dad told the story about two titans of retailing—S.S. Kresge and J.C. Penney—and with their weekly pilgrimage to my dad's lunch counter. These two men would each order a soft drink from the fountain and then unpack a sandwich and some chips from the brown paper bags they carried. They would then conduct their business meeting among the other customers who were having lunch. The unassuming gentlemen kept a low profile so they could blend in with the people around them. Part of their frugality was born out of the Depression, but they were also somewhat embarrassed by their accomplishments. While many Americans in that era were struggling to make ends meet, these two successful businessmen found it difficult to enjoy the fruits of their labor.

The guilt associated with being successful is a trait shared by many risk-takers. A relative of mine ran a large insurance brokerage, and many of his clients were small banks located in the Appalachian region of southern Ohio. Rather than drive his expensive new car when making calls, he would rent or borrow a less assuming vehicle. His theory was that the bankers would be more accommodating if he were on par with their lifestyle rather than projecting the image of a successful businessman from the big city.

He carried out this charade for several years, until one day he got a wake-up call from one of his most loyal clients. The banker informed him that although he appreciated their association, he was switching the financial institution's account to a competing firm. When queried about the change, the banker explained that the new agency was known for its innovative products, had a solid reputation, and most important, was willing to make his small bank part of their success story. The banker felt honored that they would include his institution in their growth projections and that it would be a win for both parties. Although the original agent could have offered the same arrangements, he misjudged the fact that most people like to associate themselves with winners and the success that they have created. After all, success as well as failure can be contagious.

About the Author

As the saying goes, there are three ways to make a million dollars: marry someone rich; inherit great wealth; or start with two million and invest it. Unlike most kids his age, when John turned twelve, he followed the third route. He took $100 of hard-earned money he had made from a paper route and, with help from his dad, invested it in the stock market. The security he selected was American Tobacco, considered by the experts to be a safe stock that also paid an attractive dividend. Less than a year later, the stock had lost fifty percent of its value and John realized that he could just as easily lose money as make it. He needed to gain a lot more experience and knowledge in both business and investments.

Although John was an above-average student, he always found academics somewhat boring unless he had a variety of other activities on his plate at the same time. He achieved his best grades during a semester when he was also pledging a fraternity, running track, tending bar, and spinning records as a disc jockey at a local radio station.

After graduating from college with a major in finance and economics, John enrolled in an Ohio law school. His education, however, was somewhat uneven as he was called to active duty with the Ohio Air National Guard on several occasions.

By the time he left the academic environment, he thought his studies were behind him, but in fact, they were just shifting into high gear. Joining the corporate world with a prestigious Wall Street firm, John was thrust back into the classroom for a year of intense studies about the markets he was about to enter.

He and other members of his class were not considered part of the corporate team until they had successfully completed all their assignments and demonstrated they could handle the pressures of the job. After all, the company had invested time and resources in the students' development and management was determined to get their money's worth. How the new hires conducted themselves on the job was also a reflection on the corporation and the latest members of the team were closely scrutinized by supervisors and other management.

Once he completed his courses, John had to earn passing grades on licensing exams. Although obtaining each license was a grind, the company was paying him to learn the techniques of analyzing businesses for their values and net worth, and he believed this knowledge would serve him well in the future. This thought proved to be true when he later capitalized on what he'd learned when reviewing a potential acquisition or investment for his own firm.

John stayed with the company for several years while moving steadily up the corporate ladder. The pay was good and the benefits were even better, but they came with drawbacks. His position—and those of others—were as pawns on a giant chessboard, and a career was over quickly if one did not play well with the other pieces. His manager had been transferred around the country seventeen times in the previous twenty years, and the end came for John when he was asked to replace a failing sales manager in a dead-end office in an obscure town. With a family on the way, it was time for him to put down more permanent roots.

STRADDLING THE ABYSS

Moving from Wall Street to Main Street was not a difficult adjustment, and John settled in with a small insurance brokerage and employee benefit firm located in Columbus, Ohio. With just under one hundred employees, each had the opportunity to grow with the company and secure a good future. Two partners were in charge of the operations, and although they controlled most of the stock, they put a plan in motion for the employees to buy their shares when the founders retired. All that changed a few months after John arrived, when one of the partners fell ill and passed away shortly afterward.

The surviving partner now controlled the company but seemed lost without his colleague around to help make decisions. As often happens, he turned to outside consultants for answers. Rather than follow the employee stock-purchase arrangement, he decided to protect his investment by selling out to a large East Coast insurance firm. If John stayed with the company, he would be back where he started, working for a national conglomerate, so he and a partner decided to strike out on their own and eventually created a series of successful corporate endeavors.

Studies have shown that several basic forces trigger some people to action while others choose to sit on the sidelines. The first step—biological considerations or the need for security—can motivate a person to acquire the necessities of life such as food, clothing, and shelter. The second step—economic or materialistic needs, including money, possessions, and comforts—motivate many others. After people successfully finish steps one and two, self-motivators looks to accomplish the third step: emotional security in the form of identity, status, and recognition. The final step in self-motivation is building psychic or idealistic satisfaction, which involves achieving professionalism, respect, dignity, and a compulsion to excel. Once a person has graduated from step four, he or she will have moved from fearfulness to confidence, from timidity to boldness, and from selfish desires to selfless accomplishments.

To ride out the adversities associated with risks necessary for success, an individual not only needs to be self-motivated but also have the acquired temperament and patience to deal with risk-taking behavior. Remember, as John A. Shedd mentioned, "Ships may be safe in the harbor, but that is not why ships were built."

A partner in one of John's businesses joked that when he invested, he would buy high and sell low and when his ship would finally come in, he'd be at the airport. Although what he said was an ironic comment on his investment skills, in reality his words were a true reflection of his state of mind and the actions he took.

When the stock or bond markets were nearing their lows for the year, he would dump his entire portfolio only to re-enter the arena when stocks were trending near their all-time highs. His fear of loss and his impatience, coupled with a herd mentality, was the perfect formula for monetary failure. In contrast, a measured risk-taker would subscribe to the axiom that every stock will hit a high and low for the year. To predict the date for each occurrence would be foolhardy at best, so a successful approach would be to ask, "Would I still buy this stock in today's market?" If the answer is no, then sell the losers and allow your winners to run. Losing is not part of successful investors' vocabularies. Their approach is that you win or you learn.

Like most investors who own stock in a publicly held corporation, John receives the annual report, proxy statement, and notice of the shareholder meeting. With holdings in dozens of companies, it became a formidable task for him to wade through the hundreds of pages of charts, graphs, and other statistics, in an attempt to evaluate the performance of each business for the previous year. However, over time, he has discovered a pattern that companies follow when issuing their reports that has helped him cut through the clutter and get to the vital information he is seeking.

To begin with, the first few pages of the annual report will give the stockholder a snapshot about just how much digging he or she will have to do to unravel the details of how the business has performed. Generally, if the corporation has had a profitable year, the results will be posted in bold print on the inside cover of the first page. This information would include a three-year comparison of sales volume, earnings per share, dividend history, and other valuable statistics. The chair's letter to shareholders will follow, highlighting the year's accomplishments and an upbeat vision for the future.

If the company, however, has performed poorly, shareholders seldom find the results anywhere near the front pages of the report. Instead, the chair's letter will be vague, relating to such issues as the corporate safety record, environmental impact, or a tribute to a retiring director. Thus the scavenger hunt begins as the shareholders attempt to unearth how the business really performed, which usually is buried somewhere deep inside.

Another helpful tool a stockholder can use to measure a company's achievements is the Shareholders Return Performance Graph. If he or she has invested as little as a hundred dollars, the graph traces the progress of the company vs. the S&P 500 Composite Index and an index made up of peers in a related industry for the five most completed financial years. The cumulative shareholder returns for that period, compared to the other indexes, will determine in part how well the company is doing in the marketplace and whether the shareholders are making or losing money.

Earnings per share is an important barometer in gauging how the company is progressing, but it may not tell the complete story. An increase, as compared to previous years, may be a good sign, or that increase could be misleading. Did the company have a stock buyback that reduced shares, therefore increasing the earnings ratio, or was there a one-time tax write-off that inflated the bottom line? These are areas to explore before rushing to judgment. Conversely, a decline in earnings could be the result of a short-term hiccup or the start of a more dangerous trend.

There are several things John takes into consideration when filling out his proxy vote, starting with the Board of Directors who are up for nomination. The negatives would include the number of family members serving, a lack of independent board members, or people with little experience with the company's product line who have been added to the board only for name recognition. He also looks at how much each director has invested in the company and the number of outside public boards on which they serve. When a director has a substantial number of shares, he or she is also affected by the company's performance, while a director who sits on too many outside boards probably cannot devote the time necessary to their present position.

John casts a wary eye at corporate proposals that request approval of executive compensation, stock buybacks, and long-term incentive plans. Although executive salaries may not vary much from year to year, the perks that are added, including share- and option-based awards, annual and long-term incentive plans, pension values, and all other compensation, may result in a hefty package. The fact that this compensation has little to do with the company's performance, the ratio can be hundreds if not thousands of times higher than the average worker's paycheck. This scenario generates a "no" vote from John.

Stock buybacks can be a positive sign if they are used to reduce shares, but if they are reissued to the executives in the form of stock options, the shareholder has gained nothing. The same applies to incentive plans that reward management and staff but add little value to a stock portfolio.

John takes a particular interest in shareholder proposals, which usually get a negative response from management. Positive issues, such as the call for more independent board members or reducing the number of shareholders necessary to call a special meeting, usually have merit. Some proposals, however, promote an activist agenda, pushing for environmental, social, or political changes. Although these issues may be important, it does not have a major impact on how the company generates income.

The blueprint of a company's health in the form of the annual report should not be intimidating as long as the shareholders ask the right questions and know where to look for the answers.

It has been said to enjoy a full life, a person should "plant a tree, have children, write a memoir, and take risk." Having accomplished all of these objectives, however, does not mean it is time to go into protective mode and curl up in the fetal position, waiting for the inevitable. John still stays active running businesses, overseeing investment portfolios, volunteering, and sitting on several boards. He also has a "bucket list" that is far from being completed.

Too many people work until age 65 and then retire without a purpose. They should instead retire *to* something, not *from* something, staying engaged and intellectually curious. Then, when it is time to judge one's accomplishments, they can be able to look back on their lives and say, "I have enjoyed the ride and have helped make a positive difference in the lives of others."

www.ingramcontent.com/pod-product-compliance
Lightning Source LLC
LaVergne TN
LVHW041638060526
838200LV00040B/1620